Geo. W. Matsell

# VOCABULUM;

## OR,

# THE ROGUE'S LEXICON.

COMPILED FROM THE MOST AUTHENTIC SOURCES.

BY

## GEORGE W. MATSELL,

SPECIAL JUSTICE, CHIEF OF POLICE, ETC., ETC.

THE LAWBOOK EXCHANGE, LTD.
Clark, New Jersey

ISBN-13: 9781584774846 (hardcover)
ISBN-13: 9781616190477 (paperback)

Lawbook Exchange edition 2005, 2010

*Printed in the United States of America on acid-free paper*

## THE LAWBOOK EXCHANGE, LTD.

33 Terminal Avenue
Clark, New Jersey 07066-1321

*Please see our website for a selection of our other publications
and fine facsimile reprints of classic works of legal history:*
www.lawbookexchange.com

**Library of Congress Cataloging-in-Publication Data**

Matsell, George W. (George Washington), 1811-1877.
    Vocabulum, or, The rogue's lexicon: compiled from the
most authentic sources / by George W. Matsell.
        p. cm.
Originally published: New York: G.W. Matsell & Co., 1859.
    ISBN 1-58477-484-3 (alk. paper)
1. English language—New York (State)—New York—Slang—
Dictionaries. 2. Rogues and vagabonds—New York (State)—
New York—Language—Dictionaries. 3. Americanisms—New
York (State)—New York—Dictionaries. 4. Cant—New York
(State)—New York—Dictionaries. 5. Cant—Dictionaries. I. Title:
Vocabulum. II. Title: Rogue's lexicon. III. Title.

PE3101.N7M382005
427'.974471'09034—dc22                                    2004050909

# VOCABULUM;

## OR,

# THE ROGUE'S LEXICON.

COMPILED FROM THE MOST AUTHENTIC SOURCES.

BY

## GEORGE W. MATSELL,

SPECIAL JUSTICE, CHIEF OF POLICE, ETC., ETC.

NEW-YORK:

PUBLISHED BY GEORGE W. MATSELL & CO.
PROPRIETORS OF THE NATIONAL POLICE GAZETTE.
No. 3 Tryon Row.

# PREFACE.

When a young man enters upon the business of life, he may have some indefinite idea of what he intends to follow out to the close thereof; but he soon finds himself surrounded by circumstances which control his actions and business pursuits, and lead him into channels of thought and industry that had not previously entered into his philosophy. At least I have found it to be so, and I have no doubt others have had a similar experience. To become a lexicographer, certainly never entered into my calculation, or even found a place in the castle-building of my younger days; and if a kind friend had suggested to me that I was destined to fill such a position in life, I would simply have regarded him as a fit subject for the care of the authorities. This improbable event has now taken place; and I present myself to the world as the compiler of a language used in all parts of the world, and yet understood connectedly but by few persons.

The rogue fraternity have a language peculiarly their own, which is understood and spoken by them no matter what their dialect, or the nation where they were reared. Many of their words and phrases, owing to their comprehensive meaning, have come into general use, so that a Vocabulum or Rogue's Lexicon, has become a necessity to the general reader, but more especially to those who read police intelligence.

Occupying the position of a Special Justice, and Chief of the Police of the great Metropolis of New-York, where thieves and others of a like character from all parts of the world congregate, and realizing the necessity of possessing a positive knowledge of every thing connected with the class of individuals with whom it was my duty to deal, I was naturally led to study their peculiar language, believing that it would enable me to converse with them more at ease, and thus acquire a knowledge of their character, besides obtaining from them information that would assist me in the position I occupied, and consequently be of great service to the public. To accomplish this task was no mean undertaking, as I found that it required years of diligent labor to hunt up the various authorities, and these when found proved only partially available, as much of the language in present use was unwritten, and could only be obtained by personal study among first-class thieves who had been taught it in their youth. The difficulties surrounding it, did not deter me from following out my resolution, and by closely pursuing it, I had opened up to me a fountain of knowledge that I could not have obtained if I had not possessed a clear understanding of this peculiar dialect. Experience has since demonstrated to me that any man engaged in police business can not excel without understanding the rogues' language, in the study of which they will find this Lexicon of invaluable service.

It is not, however, to policemen alone that this book will be of service, as these cant words and phrases are being interwoven with our language and many of them are becoming recognized Anglicisms. It is not unusual to see them in the messages of presidents and governors —to hear them enunciated at the bar and from the pulpit, and thus they have come to be acknowledged as appropriately expressive of particular ideas; so that while they are in common use among the footpads that infest the land, the *élite* of the Fifth Avenue pay homage to their worth, by frequently using them to express thoughts, that could not, otherwise, find a fitting representative. The vocabulary of the rogue is not of recent date; although it is mainly made up of arbitrary or technical words and phrases, while others are of a purely classical origin. It is a language of great antiquity, and may be dated back to the earliest days of the roving gipsy bands, that infested Europe, from whom the greater portion of it has been derived. It might more properly be termed the Romany or Gipsy language, adapted to the use of modern rogues in all parts of the world, and in which the etymologist will find words drawn from every known language. Some of these words are peculiarly national, but as a general thing the language of the rogue in New-York is the language of the rogue the world over.

Among policemen, not only in this city but in different parts of the United States, the cant language of thieves is attempted to be used; but there being no standard they are unable to do so understandingly, and each one gives to the words the corrupted sense in which he received it; thus speaking as it were, a miserable "*patois*," to the exclusion of the true "Parisian French." This departure from the true meaning of the words used is mischievous in its tendency, as it is calculated to mislead and bewilder, so that rogues might still converse in the presence of an officer, and he be ignorant of what they said. This I have endeavored to correct, and although I may not claim fallibility in these matters, yet I believe that I have arrived at as high a degree of perfection as is now atta'nab'e.

To the readers of the *National Polic? Gazette*, the oldest and most reliable criminal journal published in the United States, this work will prove invaluable, as it will enable them to understand and fully comprehend language that the editors and correspondents are frequently compelled to use in order to convey the idea as understood by rogues in general.

GEO. W. MATSELL.

*New-York*, 1859.

# VOCABULUM;

OR,

# THE ROGUE'S LEXICON.

————•◆•————

## A

ABRAHAM. To sham; to pretend sickness.

ABRAHAM COVE. A naked or poor man; a beggar in rags.

ACADEMY. A penitentiary, or prison for minor offenses.

ACCOUNTS. To cast accounts; to vomit.

ACE OF SPADES. A widow.

ACKRUFFS. River-thieves; river-pirates.

ACORN. A gallows.

ADAM. An accomplice; a pal.

ADAM-TILER. A fellow whose business it is to receive the plunder from the "File"—the one who picked the pocket—and get away with it.

ACTEON. A cuckold.

ACTIVE CITIZEN. A louse.

ADDLE-COVE. A foolish man.

AGOG. Anxious; impatient; all-agog.

AGOGARE. Anxious; eager; impatient; be quick.

AIR AND EXERCISE. To work in the stone quarry at Blackwell's Island or at Sing Sing.

ALAMORT. Confounded; struck dumb; unable to say or do any thing.

ALBERT. A chain.

1

ALBONIZED. Whitened.

ALLS. The five alls. First, the monarch's motto, "I govern all." Second, the bishop's motto, "I pray for all." Third, the lawyer's motto, "I plead for all." Fourth, the soldier's motto, "I fight for all." Fifth, the farmer's motto, "I pay for all."

ALTEMAL. All in a heap, without items; the sum total.

ALTITUDES. A state of drunkenness; being high.

AMBIDEXTER. One who befriends both sides; a lawyer who takes fees from both parties in a suit.

AMERACE. Very near; don't go far; be within call.

AMPUTATE YOUR MAHOGANY or TIMBER. Be off quick; away with you.

AMUSE. To amuse; to invent plausible stories and thereby rob or cheat unsuspecting persons.

AMUSERS. Fellows who carry snuff or pepper in their pockets, which they throw into a person's eyes and then run away; the accomplice rushing up to the victim, pretending to assist, robs him while suffering with pain.

ANGLERS. Small thieves who place a hook on the end of a stick, and therewith steal from store-windows, doors, etc. It also applies to fencemen; putters up, etc.

ANOINTED. Flogged.

ANKLE. "A sprained ankle;" the mother of a child born out of wedlock.

ANODYNE. Death; to anodyne, to kill. "Ahr say, Bill, vy don't yer hopen that jug and draw the cole?" "Vy, my cove, aren't you avare as how a bloke snoses hin it?" "Vell, vot hof it, aren't yer habel to put him to hanodyne?"

APPLES AND PEARS. Stairs.

AQUA. Water.

ARCH-COVES. Chief of the gang or mob; headmen; governors; presidents.

ARCH-DUKE. A funny fellow.

ARCH-GONNOFF. The chief of a gang of thieves.

ARD. Hot.

ARK. A ship; a boat; a vessel.

ARTFUL DODGERS. Lodgers; fellows who dare not sleep twice in the same place for fear of arrest.

ARTICLE. Man. "You're a pretty article." A term of contempt.

ARTICLES. A suit of clothes.

ARTIST. An adroit rogue.

ASSAY. Go on; commence; try it.

ATTLEBOROUGH. Not genuine; made to imitate. At the town of Attleborough jewelry is manufactured from the baser metals, or so alloyed as to deceive those who are not good judges of the genuine article.

AUTUM. A church.

AUTUM-BAWLER. A parson.

AUTUM-DIVERS. Pickpockets who practise in churches.

AUTUMED. Married.

AUTUM-COVE. A married man.

AUTUM-CACKLER. A married woman.

AUTUM-JET. A parson.

AWAKE. To know; to let know.

## B

BABY PAPS. Caps.

BACONNING. A fat round face; a full pale face.

BADGER. A panel thief; a fellow who robs a man's pocket after he has been enticed into bed with a woman; to torment.

BAGGED. Imprisoned.

BAG OF NAILS. Every thing in confusion.

BALLUM-RANCUM. A ball where all the dancers are thieves and prostitutes.

BALSAM. Money.

BALL. Prison allowance.

BAM. A lie; to bamboozle; humbug.

BANDOG. A civil officer.

1*

BANDERO.  A widow's weeds.

BANGUP.  The best; very fine; height of the fashion.

BAPTIZED.  Liquor that has been watered.

BARDY.  A sixpence.

BARKER.  One who patrols the streets for customers in front of his employer's shop; vide Chatham street.

BARKING.  Shooting.

BARKING-IRONS.  Pistols.

BARNACLES.  A good booty; a pair of spectacles; hand-cuffs.

BARREL FEVER.  Delirium tremens.

BASTER.  A house-thief.

BAT.  A prostitute who walks the streets only at night.

BAZAAR.  A counter.

BEAK.  A magistrate; a judge.

BEAKQUERE.  A sharp, strict magistrate who is attentive to his duty.

BEAT.  Get the best of him; "Beat the flat;" rob the man.

BEATERS.
BEATER-CASES. } Boots.

BEAU - TRAPS.  Well-dressed sharpers ; fortune-hunters.

BEANS.  Five-dollar gold-pieces.

BELCHER TIE.  A flashy neckerchief.

BEN.  A vest.

BENE.  Good; first rate.

BENE-BOUSE.  Good drink.

BENE-COVE.  A good man.

BENEN-COVE.  A better man.

BENE-CULL.  A good fellow.

BENE-DARKMAN.  Good night.

BENDER.  A spree ; a drunken frolic.

BENFLAKE.  A cheap beef-steak.

BENISON.  A blessing.

BENJAMIN.  A coat.

BENS.  Fools.

BESS.  A pick of a very simple construction.

BETSEY. *See Bess.*

BETTING HIS EYES. A term used by gamblers when a "sucker" looks on at the game, but does not bet.

BETTY. A picklock.

BEVER. An afternoon lunch.

BIENLY. Excellently, "She coaxed so bienly."

BIG THING. A rich booty.

BILBOA. A pointed instrument.

BILK. To cheat.

BILLY. A piece of whalebone or rawhide about fourteen inches long, with an oval-shaped lump of lead at each end, one larger than the other, the whole being covered with buckskin or india-rubber.

BILLY BUTTER. Mutton.

BILLY NOODLE. A soft fellow that believes the girls are all in love with him.

BILL OF SALE. A widow's weeds.

BINGO. Liquor.

BINGO-BOY. A drunken man.

BINGO-MORT. A drunken woman.

BINGAVAST. Get you gone, "Bing we to New-York;" go we to New-York.

BIRDLIME. Time. Time arrests and reveals all things.

BIRTHDAY SUIT. Stark naked.

BIT. Out-witted, "The cove was bit;" "The cove has bit the flat, and pinched his cole," outwitted and robbed him.

BIT. Done; sentenced; convicted.

BITE. To steal; to rob.

BLACK COVE-DUBBER. A turn-key; a prison keeper.

BLACK ACT. Picking locks.

BLACK-BOX. A lawyer.

BLACK FRIARS. Look out.

BLACK OINTMENT. Raw meat.

BLACK SPY. The devil.

BLACKLEG. A gambler.

BLARNEY. A picklock.

BLEAK-MORT. A pretty girl.

BLEED. To compel a person to give money under threat of exposure.

BLEAK. Handsome ; "The Moll is bleak," the girl is handsome.

BLEATING RIG. Sheep-stealing.

BLINK. Not to see when one may. "The copper blinks, and won't drop to me," i. e. the officer pretends not to see me ; the officer looks another way. To go to sleep.

BLOCK-HOUSE. A prison.

BLOWEN. The mistress of a thief. "The blowen kidded the bloke into a panel crib, and shook him of his honey and thimble," i. e. the girl enticed the man into a thieving-house, and robbed him of his watch and money.

BLOW A CLOUD. Smoke a segar or pipe.

BLOKE. A man.

BLOTTED. Written.

BLOW. To inform.

BLOSS. Woman ; mistress ; girl.

BLUDGET. A female thief who decoys her victims into alley-ways, or other dark places, for the purpose of robbing them.

BLUDGEONER. A fellow who passes off some well-dressed woman as his wife. She goes out in search of a gallant, and entices her victim into some unfrequented place. The bludgeoner waits outside until she gives him a signal that the man is robbed, when he rushes in with a knife, pistol, or club, and accuses the man with having seduced his wife. The poor fool gets away as fast as possible, and does not know that he is robbed.

BLUE-BILLY. A peculiar handkerchief.

BLUE-PIGEON-FLYING. Stealing lead off the tops of houses.

BLUE-PLUM. A bullet; "Surfeit the bloke with blue-plum," shoot him.

BLUE-RUIN. Bad gin.

BLUFF. To bluster; look big.

BLUFFER. The landlord of a hotel.

BLUNDERBUSS. An ignorant, blustering fellow.

BLUNT. Money.

BOARDING-HOUSE. City prison; the Tombs.

BOARDING-SCHOOL. Penitentiary.

BOAT. " To boat with another ;" to go in with him; to be his partner in the same boat—in the same scrape.

BOATED. Transported; gone to sea.

BOB. The fellow that carries off the plunder; a shop-lifter; a cover or staller.

BOBBIE. A policeman.

BOB-CULL. A good fellow.

BOB MY PAL. My girl.

BODY-COVER. A coat.

BOGUS. Bad coin; false.

BOKE. The nose.

BOLT. Run away.

BONE. To take; to steal; to ask him for it.

BONEBOX. The mouth.

BONED. Arrested; taken; carried off.

BONESETTER. A hard-riding horse.

BONNET. Hat. "Bonnet him," knock his hat down over his eyes.

BONNETTER. One who entices another to play; or the fellow who takes the "flat" in hand after the "roper in" has introduced him to the house.

BOOTH. A place in which thieves congregate.

BOOSING-KEN. A drinking-shop.

BOODLE. A quantity of bad money.

BOODLE-CARRIER. The man who carries the bulk of the counterfeit money that is to be passed. The person who passes, or shoves it, as it is called, hav ing but one "piece" at a time. The fellow with the boodle keeps close in the wake of the shover, to re-ceive the good money, and supply him with the counterfeit, as occasion requires.

BOOBY-HATCH. Station-house; watch-house.

BOOKED.  Arrested.
BOOLY-DOG.  An officer; a policeman.
BOOZE.  Intoxicating drink.
BORDELLO.  A house of ill-fame.
BOSHING.  A flogging.
BOTTLE-HEAD.  A stupid fellow.
BOTS.  Boots.
BOUNCE.  To scold; blow up; to swagger; to con-
vince by the force of sound more than sense.
BOUNCER.  A fellow that robs while bargaining
with the store-keeper.
BOUNCING CHEAT.  A bottle.
BOUNG.  A purse.
BOWER.  A prison.
BOWSPRIT IN PARENTHESIS.  A pulled nose.
BRACKET-MUG.  A very ugly face.
BRADS.  Money.
BRAG.  To boast.
BRASS.  Money.
BREAD-BAG.  The stomach.
BREAKUPS.  Steamboat-landings; dispersing of peo-
ple from theatres, lecture-rooms, churches, etc.
BREAK-'O-DAY DRUM.  A place for the sale of li-
quor, that never closes day or night.
BRIEF.  Duplicate.
BROADY.  Materials of any kind.
BROAD PITCHING.  The game of three-card monte.
BROADS.  Cards.
BROKEN LEG.  A woman that has had a child out
of marriage.
BROTHER OF THE BLADE.  A soldier.
BROTHER OF THE BOLUS.  A doctor.
BROTHER OF THE BUSKIN.  An actor.
BROTHER OF THE BUNG.  A brewer.
BROTHER OF THE COIF.  A counsellor-at-law.
BROTHER OF THE GUSSET.  A pimp.
BROTHER OF THE QUILL.  An author; an editor.
BROTHER OF THE STRING.  Fiddler, or musician.
BROTHER OF THE SURPLICE.  A minister.

BROTHER OF THE WHIP. A coachman.
BRUSH. To flatter; to humbug; an encounter. "It was the hardest brush I ever saw; both men were as game as pebbles. It was nothing but cut, carve, and come again."
BRUSHER. A full glass.
BRUSHING UP A FLAT. Praising or flattering.
BRUISER. A fighter.
BUBB. To drink; "Bubb your lush," drink your grog.
BUBBLE. To cheat.
BUCK. A hack-driver; bail.
BUCKET. A live man.
BUCKLER. A collar.
BUCKS-FACE. A cuckold.
BUDGE. A thief that sneaks into a store, and hides until the persons who lock up are gone, when he lets in his accomplice.
BUFE. A dog.
BUFE-NAPPER. A dog-thief; a mean rogue.
BUFFER. A pugilist.
BUFFET. A false swearer.
BUFFING IT HOME. Swearing point blank to a circumstance or thing.
BUG. A breast-pin.
BUGGING. Taking money from a thief by a policeman.
BUGABOSE. Sheriff's officers.
BUGAROCH. Handsome; very pretty.
BUGGER. A pickpocket; a buggsman.
BULL. A locomotive.
BULL-DOGS. Pistols.
BULL-TRAPS. Rogues who personate officers for the purpose of extorting money.
BULLY. A lump of lead tied in a corner of a kerchief.
BULLY TIMES. Good times.
BULK AND FILE. Shop-lifters; two pickpockets operating together—the "bulk" jostles the party that is to be robbed, and the "file" steals the treasure.

BUMMER.  A sponger.

BUMY-JUICE.  Porter or beer.

BUN.  A fellow that can not be shaken off.

BUNG.  A purse or pocket.

BURNING.  Cheating.

BURNERS.  Rogues who cheat countrymen with false cards or dice.

BURSTER.  A burglar.  Sometimes it denotes bread.

BURNT OUT.  Worn-out roués; fellows that sorrow for the past, fear the future, and can only make the present endurable through means that are revolting to human reason.

BURST.  The conclusion of an entertainment; a spree.

BUSTLED.  Confused; perplexed; puzzled.

BUS-NAPPER.  A constable.

BUST.  To enter forcibly; a burglary.

BUTTEKER.  A store.

BUTTER-KEN.  A shop or store.

BUTTERED.  Whipped.

BUTTON.  To secure; to entice a simpleton to play.

BUZZING.  Searching for.  "I was in a push and had to buzz about half a glass before I touched a flat's thimble and slang.  I fenced the swag for half a century"—"I was in a crowd and searched for half an hour before I succeeded in stealing a man's watch and chain, which I sold for fifty dollars."


# C

CAB-MOLL.  A woman that keeps a bad house.

CACKLE.  To blab.  "The cove cackles"—tells all he knows.

CAD.  A baggage-smasher; a railroad conductor.

CADGER.  A beggar; a mean thief.

CADY.  A hat.

CAG.  Sulky; morose

CAIN AND ABEL. A table.

CAKE. An easy fool of a policeman; a flat cop.

CALF-SKIN FIDDLE. A drum.

CALLE. A gown.

CAM. Cambric, "Cam wiper." Cambric kerchief.

CAMESOR. A shirt or shift.

CAN. A dollar.

CANARY-BIRD. A convict.

CANK. Dumb.

CANT. A gift; to give.

CANNIS COVE. A dog-man; a dog-merchant; a dog-thief.

CAN'T SEE. Very drunk; so that he can not see a hole through a ladder.

CAP. To join in, "I will cap in with him"—I will appear to be his friend.

CAPPER. One who supports another's assertion, to assist in cheating, "The burner bammed the flat with sham books, and his pal capped in for him"— The sharp cheated the countryman with false cards, and his confederate assisted (capped) in the fraud.

CAPER COVE. A dancing-master.

CAP BUNG. Hand it over; give it to me.

CAPTAIN HEEMAN. A blustering fellow; a coward.

CAPTAIN TOPER. A smart highwayman.

CAP YOUR LUCKY. Run away.

CARAVAN. Plenty of cash; rich; money enough.

CARLER. A clerk.

CART OF TOGS. A gift of clothes.

CARREL. Jealous.

CASA. A house, "Tout that casa"—mark that house. "It is all bob; let's dub the gig of the casa"—Now the coast is clear; let us break open the door of the house.

CASE. A dollar.

CASS. Cheese.

CASSE. A house.

2

CAST. Course, " He traversed the cast"—he walked the course.
CASTER. A cloak.
CASTOR. A hat.
CAT. A drunken prostitute; a cross old woman; a muff; a pewter pot.
CATAMARAN. An ugly woman.
CAT AND MOUSE. Keeps house, " He keeps a cat and mouse."
CATCH-POLE. A constable.
CATTER. A crowbar.
CAVED. Gave up ; surrendered.
CAXON. A wig.
CENTURY. One hundred dollars ; one hundred.
CHAFF. Humbug.
CHAFER. The treadmill.
CHAFFEY. Boisterous ; happy ; jolly.
CHAFFING. Talking ; bantering.
CHALK. To mark ; to spot.
CHALKS. To walk your chalks ; to run away.
CHALK FARM. The arm.
CHANT. Talk ; to publish ; to inform. " Give me your chant," Give me your name.
CHARLEY. A gold watch.
CHARM. A picklock.
CHAPT. Dry ; thirsty.
CHATES. Gallows.
CHANT COVES. Reporters.
CHATTS. Lice. Chatt, a louse.
CHATTY FEEDER. A spoon.
CHARLEY PRESCOT. A vest.
CHEESE. Be silent; listen. " Cheese it, the coves are fly," be silent, the people understand us.
CHERRY PIPE. A pipe ; a full-grown woman.
CHIE. Who is it? do you know ?
CHIN. A child.
CHINK. Money.
CHINKERS. Handcuffs and leg-irons united by a chain ; money.

CHIPS.  Money.

CHIVE.  A file or saw.  " Chive your darbies," file your irons off.

CHIVEY.  To scold.

CHOKER.  A neckerchief.

CHOVEY.  A shop or store.

CHOPPED UP.  When large quantities of goods are sold to a receiver, they are divided into small lots, and put into various houses, and this is called "chopping up the swag."

CHRISTENING.  Erasing the name of the maker from a stolen watch and putting another in its place.

CHURCH.  A term of endearment, " My church."

CHUMP.  Head.

CITY COLLEGE.  The Tombs.

CLANKERS.  Silver vessels.

CLARET.  Blood.

CLEAN.  Expert; smart.

CLEAR.  Run; go away; be off.

CLERKED.  Imposed upon.  " The flat will not be clerked."

CLEYMANS.  Artificial sores made by beggars to impose on the credulous.

CLICK.  A blow; a thrust.

CLICKER.  A knock down.

CLINK.  To grab; to snatch; be quick; start.

CLOUT.  Handkerchief.

CLOWER.  A basket.

CLY.  A pocket.

CLY-FAKING.  Picking pockets.

COACHWHEEL.  A dollar.

COCKED HIS TOES UP.  Dead.  " He is dead."

COCK AND HEN CLUB.  A place frequented by thieves of both sexes.

COCUM.  Sly; wary.

COFFEE.  Beans.

COG.  To cheat; to impose; a tooth.

COGLIONE.  A fool; a woman's dupe; a fop.

COLD DECK. A prepared deck of cards played on a novice or "sucker."

COLD PIG. A person that has been robbed of his clothes.

COLLAR. To seize or take.

COLLARED. Taken; arrested.

COLLEGE. A State prison.

COLLEGE CHUM. A fellow-prisoner.

COLTMAN. One who lets horses and vehicles to burglars.

COMMISTER. A parson.

COMMISSION. A shirt or shift.

COMMIT. To inform.

CONK. The nose.

CONSOLATION, Assassination. To kill a man, is to give him consolation.

CONVENIENT. A mistress.

CONFIDENCE MAN. A fellow that by means of extraordinary powers of persuasion gains the confidence of his victims to the extent of drawing upon their treasury, almost to an unlimited extent. To every knave born into the world it has been said that there is a due proportion of fools. Of all the rogue tribe, the Confidence man is, perhaps, the most liberally supplied with subjects; for every man has his soft spot, and nine times out of ten the soft spot is softened by an idiotic desire to overreach the man that is about to overreach us. This is just the spot on which the Confidence man works. He knows his subject is only a knave wrongside out, and accordingly he offers him a pretended gold watch at the price of a brass one; he calls at the front door with presents from no where, as none could be expected; he writes letters in the most generous spirit, announcing large legacies to persons who have no kin on the face of the earth who cares a copper for them. The Confidence man is perfectly aware that he has to deal with a man who expects a result without having worked for it, who gapes, and stands ready to grasp at magnificent returns. The consequence is, that the victim—the confiding man—is always *done*. The one plays a sure game; his sagacity has taught him that the great study of the mass of mankind is to get something and give nothing; but as this is bad doctrine, he wakes up out of his "brown study," and finds himself, in lieu of his fine expectations, in possession of a turnip for a watch, a cigar-box in place of a casket. The Confidence man always carries the trump card; and whoever wishes to be victimized can secure his object by making a flat of himself in a small way, while attempting to victimize somebody else.

COPPED. Arrested. "The knuck was copped to rights, a skin full of honey was found in his kick's poke by the copper when he frisked him," the pickpocket was arrested, and when searched by the officer, a purse was found in his pantaloons pocket full of money.

COPPED TO RIGHTS. Arrested on undoubted evidence of guilt.

COPBUSY. The act of handing over stolen property by a thief to one of his pals for the purpose of preventing its being found on him if arrested.

COOK. Melt; dissolve.

CORINTH. A bad house.

CORINTHIANS. Bad women who move in respectable society.

CORN-THRASHERS. Farmers.

COUPLE. To live with.

COVE or COVEY. A man.

COVER. The fellow that covers the pickpocket while he is operating.

COVING. Palming; stealing jewelry before the face and eyes of the owner, or person that is selling it.

COW. A dilapidated prostitute.

COW'S GREASE. Butter.

COW JUICE. Milk.

COWS AND KISSES. Miss, or the ladies.

2*

CRACK. To force; to burst open.

CRACKSMAN. A burglar who uses force instead of picklocks or false keys.

CRABS. Feet.

CRAB-SHELLS. Shoes.

CRAMP WORDS. Sentence of death.

CRAMPED. Killed; murdered; hanged.

CRAMMER. A falsehood.

CRAMP-RINGS. Shackles or handcuffs.

CRANKY. Mad; insane.

CRANKY-HUTCH. An insane asylum.

CRAMPING CULL. Executioner; hangman.

CRASH. To kill. "Crash that cull," kill that fellow.

CREAMY. Secretly.

CREATURE. Liquor.

CREEME. To slip money into the hands of another.

CRIB. A house.

CROAKE. To murder; to die.

CROAKED. Dead.

CROAKERS. Newspapers.

CROKUS. A doctor. "The cove sold a stiff un to a crokus for twenty cases," the rogue sold a corpse to a doctor for twenty dollars.

CROSLEITE. To cheat a friend.

CROSS. Dishonest.

CROSS-COVE. A thief; any person that lives in a dishonest way is said to be "on the cross," from the fact that highwaymen were in the habit of waiting for their victims on the cross-roads.

CROSS-DRUM. A drinking-place where thieves resort.

CROSSED. To meet another and pass him. "The swell moved as he crossed me," the gentleman bowed as he passed me.

CROSS-FANNING. Picking a pocket with the arms folded across the chest. A knuck in the front rank of a crowd desiring to steal a watch from the pocket of a gentleman standing on either side of him, first folds his arms across his breast; and pretending to be intensely looking at some object before him, stretches out the arm next his victim, and by rapid movements of his fingers and hands excites his attention, and, while in this attitude, with the hand which is stretched across his own breast, he twists the watch from the other's pocket.

CROW. The crow is the fellow that watches outside when his accomplices are inside, and gives them warning of the approach of danger.

CRUMEY. Fat; pockets full; plenty.

CRUMP. One who procures false witnesses.

CRUSHER. A policeman.

CUES. The points.

CUFFIR. A man.

CUFFIN QUEERS. Magistrates.

CULING. Snatching reticules and purses from ladies.

CULL. A man; sometimes a partner.

CUPSHOT. Drunk.

CUPBOARD LOVE. He or she loves only for what they can get.

CURLERS. Fellows who sweat gold coins by putting them in a bag, and after violently shaking, gather the dust.

CURTISONS. Broken-down lawyers; Tombs skinners.

CURBINGLAW. Stealing goods out of windows.

CUSSINE. A male.

CUT. To abandon; to renounce acquaintance; drunk; "Half cut," half drunk.

CUT BENE. Pleasant words; to speak kind.

CUTTER. A peculiar instrument that first-class screwsmen (burglars) use for cutting through iron chests, doors, etc.

CUTTING HIS EYES. Beginning to see; learning; suspicious.

CUTTY-EYED. To look out of the corner of the eyes; to look suspicious; to leer; to look askance. "The copper cutty-eyed us," the officer looked suspicious at us.

CUT UP. "The jug cut up very fat, and the gonniffs all got their regulars; there was no sinking in that mob," the bank was very rich, and the thieves all received their share; there was no cheating in that gang.

CYMBAL. A watch.

# D

DACE. Two cents.

DADDLES. Hands.

DAGAN. A sword.

DAIRY. The breasts of a woman that suckles a baby.

DAISY-ROOTS. Boots and shoes.

DAISYVILLE. The country.

DAKMA. Silence; "Dakma the bloke, and cloy his cole," silence the man, and steal his money.

DAMBER. First.

DAMBER COVE. The head man.

DANAN. Stairs.

DANCE AT HIS DEATH. To be hung; "May he dance when he dies," may he be hanged.

DANCERS. Shooting stars; fellows who do not remain long in one place.

DANCING. Sneaking up stairs to commit a larceny.

DANGLER. A roué; a seducer.

DANGLERS. A bunch of seals.

DAPPER. Well made. "The crack was dapper."

DARBIES. Handcuffs; fetters.

DARBY. Cash. "Fork over the darby," hand over the cash.

DARK CULLEY. A man who visits his mistress only at night.

DARKEY. A dark lantern. "The coves had screwed the gig of the jug, when Jack flashed the darkey into it, and found it planted full of coppers. 'Bingavast!' was the word; some one has cackled," the thieves had opened the door of a bank with false keys, and when they looked in with the aid of a dark lantern, they found the place filled with officers. One of the thieves cried out: "Be off! some one has cackled."

DAUB. A ribbon.

DAVEY. Affidavit; to witness under oath.

DAWB. To bribe. "The bene cove was scragged, because he could not dawb the beak," the good fellow was hanged, because he could not bribe the judge.

DAY-LIGHTS. The eyes.

DEAD BROKE. Not a cent.

DEAD BEAT. Without hope; certain.

DEAD GAME. A term used by gamblers when they have a certainty of winning.

DEAD TO RIGHTS. Positively guilty, and no way of getting clear.

DEAD SET. A concentrated attack on a person or thing.

DEAD SWAG. Not worth so much as it was thought to be; things stolen that are not easily disposed of.

DEATH HUNTER. The undertaker.

DEEK THE COVE. See the fellow; look at him.

DELLS. A prostitute.

DERREY. An eye-glass.

DEVIL BOOKS. Cards.

DEW-BEATERS. The feet.

DEWS. A gold eagle; ten dollars.

DIAL-PLATE. The face.

DIARY. To remember; to enter in a book. "I'L diary the joskin," I'll remember the fool.

DIB. Portion or share.

DIBS. Money.

DIDDLE. Liquor.

DIDDLE COVE. A landlord.

DIE. Dummy, or pocket-book.

DIFT COVE. A neat little man.

DIGGERS. Finger-nails.

DIMBER. Handsome; pretty

3

DIMBER-MORT. Pretty girl; enchanting girl.

DING. To throw away; to strike.

D. I. O. Damn it! I'm off.

DIP. A kiss in the dark; a pickpocket.

DIP. To pick a pocket; the act of putting a hand into a pocket.

DIPT. Pawned.

DISMAL DITTY. The psalm or hymn sung by persons just before they are hanged.

DISPATCH. A mittimus; a warrant of arrest.

DIVER. A pickpocket.

DIVING. Picking pockets.

DIVING-BELL. A rum-shop in a basement.

DOASH. A cloak.

DOBING LAY. To steal from stores early in the morning. Two thieves enter a store, as soon as the porter opens it; one of them inquires about some goods he pretends he was looking at the day before, and wishes to see them. The goods inquired for are either in the back of the store or up stairs. In the absence of the porter, the other fellow robs the store.

DOCTORS. False cards or dice.

DOCTOR GREEN. A young inexperienced fellow.

DOG-NIPPERS. Rogues who steal dogs, and restore them to their owners after a reward has been offered.

DOGS-PASTE. Sausage-meat; mince-meat.

DOING POLLY. Picking oakum in prison.

DOLLY SHOP. A loan office.

DOMESTIC. Made at home. The man robbed himself; some one in the house assisted the thieves. "You may look at home for the thief."

DOMMERER. A fellow that pretends to be deaf and dumb.

DONE. Convicted.

DONKEY-RIDING. Cheating in weight or measure; miscounting.

DONNEZ. To give.

DOPEY.  A thief's mistress.

DOOKIN COVE.  A fortune-teller.

DOSE.  Burglary.

DOSS.  A bed.  "The badger got under the doss, and frisked the bloke's pokes of two centuries and a half, and then bounced the flat till he mizzled."

DOTS.  Money.

DOWN.  Hatred; dislike; vindictive; to suspect another.  "The copper cutty-eyed me and measured my mug, and is down on the job," the officer looked at me from the corners of his eyes, and examined my face; he suspects what we are about.

DOWNEY.  A smooth, pleasant talker; a knowing fellow.

DOWNER.  A five cent piece.

DOWSE.  To strike.  "Dowse his mug." hit his face.

DONBITE.  A street.

DOXIE.  A girl.

DRAB.  A nasty woman.

DRAG.  A cart or wagon.

DRAGGING.  Stealing from shop-doors.

DRAGONS.  Sovereigns; gold coins.

DRAGSMAN.  A thief that steals from express wagons and carts; also trunks from the back of coaches.  They sometimes have a fast horse and light wagon.

DRAY.  Three.

DRAW. ⎫ Picking pockets.  "I say, my kinchin, what's your lay?"  "Vy, yer see,
DRAWING. ⎭ as how I am learning to draw."

DROMEDARY.  A clumsy, blundering fellow.

DROPS, or DROPPERS.  Fellows that cheat countrymen by dropping a pocket-book filled with bad money, near their heels, and then pretend that they found it.  By the aid of an accomplice, the countryman is induced to purchase it, with the avowed intention of finding the real owner, believing it to contain good money.

DROPT DOWN.  Low-spirited.  "The kiddy dropt

down when he went to be scragged," the youngster was very low-spirited when he walked out to be hanged.

DRUM. A drinking-place.

DRUMSTICK. A club.

DRY UP. Be silent; stop that.

DUB LAY. Robbing houses by picking the locks.

DUB. A key; a picklock.

DUCE. Two cents; two.

DUB O' THE HICK. A blow on the head. The copper tipt the dromedary a dub o' the hick with his drum-stick.

DUB THE JIGGER. Open the door.

DUBLER. A picker of locks.

DUDS. Clothes.

DUFF. Pudding.

DUFFER. A fellow, in the dress of a sailor, who knocks at the basement-door, and inquires if the lady of the house does not want to buy some smuggled goods, and then exhibits imitation silks, satins, Irish linens, etc., etc., which he pretends to have run ashore without the knowledge of the custom-house officers.

DUKES. The hands.

DUMMY. A pocket-book; a portmonnaie. "Frisk the dummy of the screens, ding it and bolt; they are crying out beef," take out the money and throw the pocket-book away; run, they are crying, stop thief!

DUN. A *very importunate* creditor. Dunny, in the provincial dialect of several counties in England, signifies *deaf;* to dun, then, perhaps may mean to deafen with *importunate demands;* it may have been derived from the word *donnez*, which signifies *give.* But the word undoubtedly originated in the days of one Joe Dun, a famous bailiff of the town of Lincoln, England, who was so extremely active and dexterous in his business, that it became a proverb, when a man refused to pay, to say, "Why

don't you Dun him?" that is, send Dun after him. Hence it became a cant word, and is now as old as the days of Henry VII. Dun was also the name for the hangman, before that of Jack Ketch.

> " And presently a halter got,
>   Made of the best strong hempen teer,
>   And ere a cat could lick her ear,
>   Had tied it up with as much art,
>   As DUN himself could do for's heart."
>           *Cotton's Virgil Trav.*   Book **IV.**

DUNNAKIN.   It can't be helped; necessary.
DUNNOCK.   A cow.
DUNEKER.   A thief that steals cattle.
DUNNEY.   Deaf; to dun.
DURIA.   Fire.
DUSTMAN.   Dead man.   "Poor Bill is a dustman; he was a bene cove," poor Bill is dead; he was a good man.
DUSTY.   Dangerous.   "Two fly-cops and a beak tumbled to us, and Bill thought as how it was rather dusty, and so, shady was the word," two detectives and a magistrate came upon us suddenly; Bill said it was rather dangerous, and so we got out of sight.

## E

EARTH-BATH.   A grave.
EASE.   To rob.
EASE THE COVE.   Rob the man.
EASON.   To tell.
EASY.   Killed.   "Make the cull easy," kill him; gag him.
EAT.   To take back; to recall; to retract; to unsay.
EAVES.   A hen-roost; a poultry-house.
EAVESDROPPER.   A mean fellow; a petty larceny vagabond.
EDGE.   Encourage; persuade; induce.

3*

EGROTAT.   He is sick.

ELBOW.   Turn the corner; get out of sight.

ELBOW-SHAKER.   A man that gambles with dice.

ELEPHANT.   The fellow has an enormous booty, and knows not how to secrete it.   If he had less, he would be able to save more.

ELFEN.   Walk light; on tiptoe.

EMPEROR.   A drunken man.

ENGLISH BURGUNDY.   London porter.

EQUIPT.   Rich; full of money; well dressed, "The cull equipped me with a deuce of finifs," the man gave me two five-dollar bills.

ERIFFS.   Young thieves; minor rogues.

ETERNITY-BOX.   A coffin.

EVERLASTING.   The treadmill.

EVIL.   A wife; a halter; matrimony.

EWE.   An old woman dressed like a young girl, "An old ewe dressed lamb fashion."   "A white ewe," a beautiful woman.

EXECUTION-DAY.   Wash-day; cleaning house.

EYE.   Nonsense; humbug.

# F

FACER.   A glass filled so full that there is no room for the lip; a staller, or one who places himself in the way of persons who are in hot pursuit of his accomplices.

FADGE.   It won't do, "It won't fadge."

FAG.   A lawyer's clerk; to beat.   "Fag the flat," beat the fool.

FAGGER.   A small boy put into a window to rob the house, or to open it for others to rob.

FAGGOT.   To bind.   "Faggot the culls," bind the men.

FAIKING.   Cutting out the wards of a key.

FAITHFUL.   A tailor that gives long credit.   "I say, Sam, what kind of crib was that you cracked?" "Oh! it belonged to one of the faithful."

FAKEMENT. A written or printed paper; the written deposition of a witness.

FAKER. A jeweller.

FAM GRASP. To shake hands. "Fam grasp the cove," shake hands with the fellow.

FAMILY-MAN. A receiver of stolen goods from a dwelling-house.

FAMLY-MAN. Connected with thieves.

FAM LAY. Thieves who rob jewellers' stores by pretending to want to make a purchase.

FAMS. Hands.

FAN. A waistcoat.

FANNY BLAIR. The hair.

FARMER. An alderman.

FASTNER. A warrant.

FAT. Money.

FATERS. Fortune-tellers.

FEEDERS. Silver spoons or forks. "Nap the feeders," steal the spoons.

FEKER. Trade; profession.

FEINT. A pawn-broker.

FEN. A common woman.

FENCE. A receiver of stolen goods; to sell stolen goods. "The bloke fenced the swag for five cases," the fellow sold the plunder for five dollars.

FENCED. Sold.

FERM. A hole.

FIB. To beat. "Fib the bloke's quarron in the rumpad, and draw the honey in his poke," beat the fellow's carcase in the street, and steal the money in his pocket.

FIBBING. Striking with the fist.

FIDLAM BENS. Thieves who have no particular lay, whose every finger is a fish-hook; fellows that will steal any thing they can remove.

FIDLAM COVES. Small thieves who steal any thing they can lay hands on.

FIGDEAN. To kill.

FIGGER. A juvenile thief put through side-lights at

outside doors to unbolt the door and admit other thieves to the house.

FIGNER. A small thief.

FIGGING LAW. The art of picking pockets.

FIGURE-DANCER. One who alters the numbers or figures on bank-bills.

FILE. A pick-pocket. The file is one who is generally accompanied by two others, one of whom is called the "Adam tyler;" and the other the "bulker,' or "staller." It is their business to jostle, or "ramp" the victim, while the "file" picks his pocket and then hands the plunder to the Adam tyler, who makes off with it.

FINE. Imprisoned. "The cove had a fine of two stretchers and a half imposed upon him for relieving a joskin of a load of cole," the fellow was sentenced to imprisonment for stealing a countryman's money.

FINGER-BETTER. A fellow who wants to bet on credit, and indicates the favorite card by pointing to it with his finger.

FINNIFF. Five dollars.

FIRE. Danger. "This place is all on fire; I must pad like a bull or the cops will nail me," every body is after me in this place; I must run like a locomotive or the officers will arrest me.

FISH. A seaman.

FITTER. A fellow that fits keys to locks for burglars.

FIZZLE. To escape. "The cove made a fizzle," the fellow escaped.

FIZZLED. Broke up; fell through.

FLAG ABOUT. A low strumpet.

FLAM. To humbug. "Flam the bloke," humbug the fellow.

FLAME. A mistress.

FLAPPERS. Hands.

FLASH. Knowing; to understand another's meaning; to "patter flash," to speak knowingly.

FLASH - DRUM. A drinking-place resorted to by thieves.

FLASH-HOUSE. A house of resort for thieves.

FLASH-KEN. A thieves' boarding-house.

FLASH-MAN. A fellow that has no visible means of living, yet goes dressed in fine clothes, exhibiting a profusion of jewelry about his person.

FLASH YOUR IVORY. Laugh; show your teeth.

FLASH HER DILES. Spend her money.

FLASH PANNY. A house resorted to by rogues of both sexes.

FLAT. A man that is not acquainted with the tricks and devices of rogues.

FLATTER-TRAP. The mouth.

FLAWED. Half-drunk; quick-tempered; not exactly honest.

FLAY. To vomit.

FLESH-BROKER. A match maker; a procuress.

FLICKER. To drink. "Flicker with me," drink with me.

FLICKERING. Laughing; smiling; drinking.

FLICKING. Cutting. "Flick me some panam and caffar," cut me some bread and cheese. "Flick the Peter and rake the swag, for I want to pad my beaters," cut the portmanteau and divide the plunder, I want to walk my boots, (to be off.)

FLIMP. To tussel; to wrestle.

FLIMPING. Garroting; highway robbery.

FLIMSEY. A bank-note.

FLING. To get the best of another. "The sharp will fling the bloke," the rogue will cheat the man.

FLOORERS or TRIPPERS. Fellows that cause persons to slip or fall in the street, and then, while assisting them up, steal their watch or portmonnaie. They are sometimes called "rampers." A gentleman in a hurry on his way to the bank, or any other place of business, is suddenly stopped by a fellow directly in front of him, going in an opposite direction to himself, who has apparently slipped or stumbled, and in endeavoring to save himself from falling, thrusts his head into the pit of the gentleman's stomach, thereby knocking him down. Immediately two very kind gentlemen, one on each side, assist him to rise, and when on his feet busy themselves in brushing the dirt from his clothing, during which operation they pick his pockets. Thanking his kind assistants with much profuseness, he goes on his way, and very soon afterwards finds himself minus his watch or pocket-book, and perhaps both.

**FLUE-SCRAPERS.** Chimney-sweeps.

**FLUSH.** Plenty; the cove.

**FLUTE.** The recorder of a city.

**FLUX.** To cheat; cozen; over-reach.

**FLY.** Knowing; up to him. "The bloke was fly, and I could not draw his fogle," the man was aware of what I wanted, and I could not steal his handkerchief.

**FLY-COP.** Sharp officer; an officer that is well posted; one who understands his business.

**FLYERS.** Shoes.

**FLYING COVES.** Fellows who obtain money by pretending to persons who have been robbed, that they can give them information that will be the means of recovering their lost goods.

**FLYING JIGGERS.** Turnpike-gates.

**FOB.** To cheat.

**FOG.** Smoke.

**FOGLE.** A pocket-handkerchief.

**FOGLE-HUNTING,** Stealing pocket-handkerchiefs.

**FOGRAM.** A fusty old fellow.

**FOGUE.** Fierce; fiery; impetuous.

**FOGUS.** Tobacco. "Tip me a gage of fogus," give me a cigar, or a pipe and tobacco.

**FORK.** A pickpocket.

**FORKS.** The fore and middle fingers.

**FOXEY.** Cunning; crafty; sly.

**FOXING.** To pretend to be asleep.

FOYST.   A cheat.

FOYSTER.   A pickpocket.

FRAMER.   A shawl.

FREE.   To steal.

FRENCH CREAM.   Brandy—called "French cream,"
  by the old Tabbies, when mixed with their tea.

FRIDAY.   Hangman's day.

FRIDAY FACE.   A dismal countenance; the face of
  a man who is sentenced to be executed.

FRISK.   To search; to examine.

FROG.   A policeman.

FROG AND TOE.   The city of New-York.   "Coves,
  let us frog and toe," coves, let us go to New-York.

FRUMPER.   A sturdy blade.

FUBSEY.   Plump.

FUBSEY DUMMEY.   A fat pocket-book.

FULLIED.   Committed for trial.

FUMBLES.   Gloves.

FUN.   To cheat.   "To fun a man," is to cheat him.

FUNK.   To frighten.

FUNKED OUT.   Frightened; backed out.

FUNKERS.   The very lowest order of thieves.

FUSSOCK.   An old fat woman.

FUSTIAN.   Wine.

## G

GABS.   Talk.

GABBEY.   A foolish fellow.

GADDING THE HOOF.   Going without shoes.

GAFF.   A theatre; a fair.   "The drop-coves maced
  the joskins at the gaff," the ring-droppers cheated
  the countrymen at the fair.

GAFFING.   Tossing; pitching; throwing.

GAGE.   Man; fellow.   "Deck the gage," see the
  man.

GAGERS.   Eyes.

GAIT.   Manner; fashion; way; profession.   "I say,
  Tim, what's your gait now?"   "Why, you see, I'm
  on the crack," (burglary.)

GALENA. Salt pork.

GALIGASKIN. A pair of breeches.

GAM. Stealing.

GAME. The particular line of rascality the rogue is engaged in; thieving; cheating.

GAMMON. To deceive. "What rum gammon the old sharp pitched into the flat," how finely the knowing old fellow flattered the fool.

GAMMY. Bad.

GAN. The mouth or lips.

GANDER. A married man not living at home with his wife.

GANG. Company; squad; mob.

GAPESEED. Wonderful stories; any thing that will cause people to stop, look, or listen.

GARRET. The head.

GARRETTING. To rob a house by entering it through the scuttle or an upper window.

GARROTE. To choke.

GARROTERS. Fellows that rob by choking their victim. Three fellows work together in this manner: The tallest of the three steps behind the victim, and putting his right arm around the neck, compresses the windpipe, and at the same time, locks the right leg by throwing his own around it. Another of the confederates secures his hands, while the third rifles his pockets. Should the garroting be done on a public thoroughfare, where people are passing, the garroters engage in laughter and jocular remarks, as if it were a pleasant lark among friends. They sometimes sprinkle rum on and about the victim's neck and face, so as to induce persons who find him, after they have left him half-dead and stupified, to believe that he is drunk.

GATTER. Drink of any kind.

GELTER. Money.

GERMAN FLUTE. A pair of boots.

GETAWAY. A locomotive; railroad train.

GHOULS. Fellows who watch assignation-houses, and

follow females that come out of them to their homes
and then threaten to expose them to their husbands,
relatives, or friends, if they refuse to give them not
only money, but also the use of their bodies.

GIG. A door. "Dub the gig of the cosa," break
open the door of the house.

GIGG. A nose. "Snitchel the bloke's gigg," smash
the man's nose.

GIGGER. A lock or door. "Dub the gigger," open
the door.

GIGGER-DUBBER. A turn-key; a prison-keeper.

GIG-LAMPS. A pair of spectacles.

GILFLIRT. A proud, capricious woman.

GILL. A woman.

GILT or JILT. A crowbar.

GILT-DUBBER. A hotel-thief.

GILYORE. Plenty.

GINGERLY. Cautiously.

GIP. A thief.

GLASS. An hour. "The badger piped his Moll
about a glass and a half before she cribbed the flat."

GLAZE. Break the glass. "I say, Bill, you mill the
glaze, and I'll touch the swag and mizzle," I say,
Bill, you break the glass, and I will steal the goods
and run away.

GLAZIER. A fellow that breaks windows or show-
cases, to steal the goods exposed for sale.

GLIB. Smooth; polite. "The bloke is glib," the
fellow is polite.

GLIBE. Writing; a written agreement.

GLIMS. Eyes.

GLIMSTICKS. Candlesticks.

GLIM FLASHY. In a passion; savage.

GLIMMER. The fire.

GLUM. Sombre; low-spirited.

GLUTTON. A fellow that can stand a great deal of
beating.

GNOSTICS. Knowing ones; smart fellows; sharps.

GNARLER. A little dog, who, by his barking, alarms

4

the family. Gnarlers are more feared by burglars than guns or pistols.

GOAWAYS. Railroad trains. "The knuck was working the goaways at Jersey City, and had but just touched a bloke's leather, as the bull bellowed for the last time, and so the cove mizzled through the jigger. The flat roared beef; but it was no go, as the bull was going very mad," the pickpocket was busy in the cars at Jersey City, and had just stolen a man's pocket-book, as the locomotive blew its whistle for the last time. The thief bolted through the door, and off the cars, just as the victim had discovered his loss and cried, " stop thief!" But it was of no avail, as the locomotive was going very fast.

GO. The fashion. " All the go," all the fashion.

GOADS. Peter Funks; cappers in.

GO BACK. To turn against. "He won't go back on the cove ; he is staunch," he will not turn against the fellow, for he is a true man.

GOATER. Dress.

GOB. The mouth.

GOBSTICKS. Silver forks or spoons.

GOBSTRING. A bridle.

GODFATHERS. Jurymen; so called because they name the degrees of crime as to grand or petit larceny, etc., etc.

GOLDFINCH. Gold coin.

GONNOFF. A thief that has attained the higher walks of his profession.

GOOH. A prostitute.

GOREE. Gold dust.

GORGER. A gentleman; a well-dressed man.

GOOSECAP. A silly fellow ; a fool.

GOOSEBERRY-LAY. Stealing wet clothes from clothes-lines or bushes.

GOOSEBERRY-PUDDING. Woman.

GOOSING SLUM. A brothel.

GOT HIM DOWN CLOSE. Know all about him; know where to find him.

**GOT HIM DOWN FINE.** Know for a certainty; Know all his antecedents.

**GO THE JUMP.** Sneak into a room through the window.

**GOVERNOR'S STIFF.** A governor's pardon.

**GRABBED.** Arrested.

**GRABBLE.** To seize. "You grabble the goose-cap and I'll frisk his pokes," you seize the fool, and I'll search his pockets.

**GRAFT.** To work.

**GRAFTING.** Working; helping another to steal.

**GRASSVILLE.** The country.

**GREASE.** A bribe. "Grease the copper in the fist, and he'll be as blind as your mother," put money in the officer's hand, and he will not watch you.

**GREED.** Money.

**GRIG.** A merry fellow.

**GRIM.** Death; "Old Grim."

**GRIN.** A skeleton.

**GRIPE-FIST.** A broker; a miser.

**GROANERS.** Thieves who attend at charity sermons, and rob the congregation of their watches and purses, exchange bad hats for good ones, steal the prayer-books, etc., etc.

**GROGHAM.** A horse.

**GROPERS.** Blind men.

**GROUND SWEAT.** A grave.

**GRUEL.** Coffee.

**GRUNTER.** A country constable.

**GUMMEY-STUFF.** Medicine.

**GUN.** To watch; to examine; to look at.

**GUN.** A thief.

**GUNNED.** Looked at; examined. "The copper gunned me as if he was fly to my mug," the officer looked at me as if he knew my face.

**GUNPOWDER.** A scolding or quick-tempered woman.

**GUNS.** Pickpockets.

**GUERRILLAS.** This name is applied by gamblers to

fellows who skin suckers when and where they can, who do not like the professional gamblers, but try to beat them, sometimes inform on them, and tell the suckers that they have been cheated.

GUTTER. Porter.

GUTTER-LANE. The throat.

GUY. A dark lantern.

## H

HACKUM. A bravado; a slasher. "Capt. Hackum," a fellow who slashes with a bowie-knife.

HALF-A-HOG. A five-cent piece.

HALF-A-NED. A five-dollar gold piece.

HALF-A-STRETCH. Six months' imprisonment.

HAMLET. A captain of police.

HAMS. Pants.

HANDLE. Nose. "The cove flashed a rare handle to his physog." The fellow has a very large nose.

HANG BLUFF. Snuff.

HANG IT UP. Think of it; remember it.

HANG OUT. The place one lives in. "The cops scavey where we hang out," the officers know where we live.

HANGMAN'S DAY. Friday is so called from the custom of hanging people on a Friday.

HANK. To know something about a man that is disreputable. "He has a hank on the bloke whereby he sucks honey when he chooses," he knows something about the man, and therefore induces him to give him money when he chooses.

HARD. Metal.

HARD COLE. Silver or gold money.

HARDWARE. False coin.

HARE IT. Return; come back.

HARMAN. A constable.

HARMAN BEAK. The sheriff.

HARP. A woman.

HARRIDAN. A haggard old woman; a scold.

HASH. To vomit.
HATCHES. In distress; in trouble; in debt.
HAWK. A confidence man; a swindler.
HAVIL. A sheep.
HAVEY CAVEY. Wavering; doubtful.
HEAVE. To rob. "To heave a crib," to rob a house.
HEAVER. The breast or chest of a person.
HEAVERS. Persons in love.
HEAVING. Stealing; taking. "The cove was done for heaving a peter from a cart," the fellow was convicted for stealing a trunk from a cart.
HEDGE. To bet on both sides; to be friends with both sides; to pray "Good God," "Good Devil."
HEELS. To run away.
HEELER. An accomplice of the pocket-book dropper. The heeler stoops behind the victim, and strikes one of his heels as if by mistake; this draws his attention to the pocket-book that lies on the ground.
HEMP. To choke.
HEMP THE FLAT. Choke the fool.
HEN. A woman.
HERRING. All bad; all alike.
HICKEY. Tipsy; not quite drunk; elated.
HICKJOP. A fool.
HICKSAM. A countryman; a fool.
HIGH BEAK. The first judge; the president; the governor; the head official.
HIGHFLYER. An audacious, lewd woman.
HIGH BLOKE. A well-dressed fellow.
HIGH GAG. Telling secrets; a fellow that whispers.
HIGH JINKS. Small gamblers.
HIGH-LIVER. A fellow who lives in a garret.
HIGH PADS. Highway robbers.
HIGH ROPES. In a passion; very loud.
HIGH TIDE. Plenty of money.
HIGH TOBERS. Gonnoffs; the highest order of thieves, who generally go well dressed, and frequent watering-places, etc., etc.

4*

HIGH TOBY. A highway robber.

HIKE. Run away. "Hike; the cops have tumbled to us," run; the officers have seen us.

HIP INSIDE. Inside coat-pocket.

HIP OUTSIDE. Outside coat-pocket.

HISTORY OF THE FOUR KINGS. A pack of cards. "The bloke's skin is lathy, he studies the history of the four kings closer than the autum-bawler's patter," the man's purse is thin; he studies a pack of cards more than the parson's sermons.

HOCK. Caught in hock; caught by the heels. "If the cove should be caught in the hock he won't snickle," if the fellow should be caught in the act, he would not tell.

HOCKEY. Drunk.

HOCKS. The feet.

HOCUS. To stupify. "Hocus the bloke's lush, and then frisk his sacks," put something into the fellow's drink that will stupify him, and then search his pockets.

HOBB. A country-fellow.

HOBINOL. A clown.

HOBNAIL. A countryman.

HOB OR NOB. What will you drink?

HOD. A mason; a builder.

HOG IN ARMOR. A blustering office-holder.

HOG IN TOGS. A well-dressed loafer.

HOGO. High-flavored; strong-scented.

HOGG. A ten-cent piece.

HOGGING. To humbug.

HOIST. To rob houses by climbing into a window. It is generally done by two or three fellows, one of whom stands close to the house, and the others climb up on him to the window.

HOISTER. A shop-lifter.

HOISTING. Putting a man upright on his head, and shaking him until his money and watch fall out of his pockets; they hold this to be no robbery.

HOISTLAY. *See Hoist.*

HOLLOW. Certain; a decided beat.

HONEY. Money.

HOODY-DOODY. A short clump of a person.

HOOF. Foot. "To beat the hoof," to travel on foot.

HOOKED. To steal.

HOOKER. A thief.

HOOP. A ring.

HOOP IT. Run away.

HOP THE TWIG. Be off; go off.

HOPPED THE TWIG. Hung.

HORNESS. Watchman.

HORSE-CAPPERS. Fellows that cheat simple people out of their money by the aid of a broken-down first-class horse.

HOSTEL. A tavern.

HOT. Too well known. "The cove had better move his beaters into Dewsville, it is too hot for him here; if he stops, he'll be sure to be sick for twenty stretches," the fellow had better go into the country, for if he stays, he will be sent to prison for twenty years.

HOUSE TO LET. A widow's weeds.

HUBBUB. Pain in the stomach.

HUE. Lash him.

HUEY. The National Police Gazette.

HUFF. A bullying, cowardly fellow.

HUG. To choke.

HUGGING THE HOOKER. Choking the thief.

HUMBOX. An auctioneer's rostrum.

HUMMER. A great lie.

HUMPHREY. A coat used by pickpockets, that has pocket-holes, but no pockets.

HUSH. Murder. "Hush the bloke," kill the fellow.

HUSH-STUFF. Money given to prevent a witness from testifying.

## I

ICKEN.　Oak.

ICKEN BAUM.　An oak-tree.

IDEA-POT.　A man's head.

IMPOST-TAKER.　One who lends money to thieves and gamblers at very high rates.

IMPUDENT.　To cut the tails of a man's coat.

IMPURE.　A lady of easy virtue.

INDORSER.　One who flogs another on the back.

INGLERS.　Horse-dealers who cheat those that deal with them.

INKLE.　Let him know.

INLAID.　Plenty of money saved.

INNOCENT.　A corpse.

INNOCENTS.　Convicts, because it is supposed that they can not commit crime.

INSIDER.　One who knows.

INTIMATE.　A shirt.　"Intimate as your shirt."

IRON.　Courage; fearless; staunch.

IRON DOUBLET.　Innocence; not guilty.

IRONED.　Handcuffed.

IVY BUSH.　A very small-faced man who has a large quantity of hair on his face and head.

IVORIES.　The teeth.　"How the blowen flashes her ivories," how the girl shows her teeth.

## J

JABBER.　To talk in an unknown language.

JACK.　A small coin.

JACK COVE.　A mean low fellow.

JACK DANDY.　A little impertinent fellow.

JACKED.　Lamed.

JACKET.　To show one up; point one out.　The fly cops pulled him, and allowed the flat cops to jacket him; so you see it was dusty for him, and I advised him to pike into Daisyville for a few moons until the down blew off.

JACK-GAGGER. A fellow that lives on the prostitution of his wife.

JACK KETCH. The hangman. This cognomen for
the hangman is of very ancient date. In the year
1682, we find in "Butler's Ghost," p. 54, the following lines:

> "Till Ketch observing he was choused,
> And in his province much abused;
> In open hall the tribute dunned,
> To do his office, or refund."

Jack Ketch had not been long appointed to his
office; for we find the name of his predecessor
(Dun) in the former part of this poem,

> "For you, yourself, to act Squire Dun,
> Such ignominy ne'er saw the sun."

The addition of "Squire" to Dun's name was an
evidence that he had executed some state criminal,
which, according to the custom of the times, ac-
corded to him that title. The predecessor of Dun
was one Gregory; from whom the gallows was
called the "Gregorian tree," and by which name it
is mentioned in the prologue to "Mercurius Prag-
maticus," tragi-comedy, acted in 1641:

> "This trembles under the black rod, and he
> Doth fear his fate from the Gregorian tree."

Gregory succeeded Derrick, who flourished in the
year 1608, as we find in an old book of that time:
"For he rides his circuit with the devil, and Derrick must be his host, and Tyburn the inne at which
he will light." "At the gallows where I leave them,
as to the haven at which they must all cast anchor,
if Derrick's cables do but hold."

JACOB. A ladder.

JACOBITE.  A shirt-collar.
JACK OF LEGS.  A very tall fellow.
JACK-RUN.  A license.
JACK SPRAT.  A small fellow.
JACK WRIGHT.  A fat fellow.
JADE.  A long term of imprisonment.
JAGGER.  A gentleman.
JAGUE.  A cut; a ditch.
JAM.  A gold ring.
JAMMED.  Killed; murdered; hanged.
JANASMUG.  A go-between; one who goes between
the thief and the fence.
JANAZARIES.  A mob of pickpockets.
JAPANNED.  A convict is said to be japanned when
the chaplain pronounces him to be converted.
JARK.  A seal.
JARKMAN.  One who writes characters for servants,
begging petitions, etc., etc.
JARVEY.  A driver.
JASKER.  A seal.
JAW COVES.  Auctioneers, lawyers.
JAZEY.  A man with an enormous quantity of hair
on his head and face.
JEFFEY.  Lightning.
JEM.  A gold ring.
JENNEY.  A hook on the end of a stick.
JENNY LINDA.  A window, pronounced *winder*.
JERRY.  A chamber-pot.
JERRY-SNEAK.  A hen-pecked husband.
JESSANY.  A man well dressed.
JET AUTUM.  A parson.
JEW'S-EYE.  A pleasant, agreeable sight.
JIG.  A trick.
JIGGER.  A door.  "Dub the jigger," open the door.
JILT.  A prostitute who hugs and kisses a country-
man while her accomplice robs him.
JILTER.  A sneak-thief.
JINGLEBRAINS.  A wild, thoughtless fellow.
JOB.  A robbery.  "To do a job," to commit a rob-
bery.

JOB. Patience; take time; don't be in a hurry.

JOBATION. A reproof; painful.

JOBBER-NOT. A tall, ungainly fellow.

JOB'S DOCK. An hospital. "The poor cove is in Job's dock," the poor fellow is in the hospital.

JOCK. Enjoy; to enjoy any thing.

JOCKUM GAGE. A chamber-pot.

JOEY. A hypocrite. Sometimes, four.

JOLLY. The head ; an excuse; a pretense.

JOMER. A mistress.

JORDAN. Disagreeable; hard to be done.

JORDAIN. A blow. "I'll tip the Jack Cove a jordain on the jazey, if I transnear him," I'll hit the mean fellow with my club on his big nose, if I get near him.

JOSEPH. A coat that's patched; a sheepish, bashful fellow.

JOSEPH'S COAT. Guarded against temptation. "I say, my bene blowen, can't you kiddy the bloke?" "No, Dick, it's of no use trying, he wears a Joseph's coat," I say, my good girl, can't you seduce the man? No, Dick, its no use trying, he is guarded against temptation.

JOSKIN. A countryman; a silly fellow. "The cove maced the joskin of twenty cases," the fellow cheated the countryman out of twenty dollars.

JUG. A bank.

JUMP. A widow; run away.

JUMPED HIS BAIL. Run away from his bail.

JUMPERS. Fellows that rob houses by getting into windows.

JURK. A seal.

## K

KATE. A smart, brazen-faced woman.

KATEY. A picklock.

KEELER. A small tub, or firkin.

KEFFEL. A horse.

KELTER.  Condition; order.

KE-KEYA.  Devil; Satan.

KEN.  A house.  "Bite the ken," rob the house.

KEN-CRACKER.  A house-breaker.

KETCH.  Hang.  "I'll ketch you," I'll hang you.

KICK.  A pocket.  "The Moll stubbled her skin in her kick," the woman held her purse in her pocket.

KICK-CLOY.  A pair of breeches.

KICKSIES.  Pants; breeches.

KICKED THE BUCKET.  Dead.

KID.  A child; a youth; a young one.

KIDDED.  Coaxed; amused; humbugged.  "The sneaksman kidded the cove of the crib, while his pal tapped the till," the thief amused the store-keeper, while his comrade robbed the money-drawer.

KIDDIES.  Young thieves.

KIDDEN.  A boy lodging-house.

KIDMENT.  Comical.

KIDSMAN.  A fellow that boards and lodges boys for the purpose of teaching them how to steal, putting them through a course of training, as a dog-trainer will train dogs for the hunt.  The kidsman accompanies the kid, and though committing no depredations himself, he controls and directs the motions of the others.

KIDNEY.  The same kind.

KILL DEVIL.  New rum.

KIMBAW.  To bully; to beat.  "Let's kimbaw the bloke," let us bully or beat the fellow.

KINCHIN.  A young child.

KINCHIN COVES.  Boys taught how to steal.

KINCHIN MORTS.  Girls educated to steal.

KIP.  A bed; half a fool.

KIRJALIS.  Who fears? I fear not; come on.

KIRKBUZZER.  A fellow that picks pockets in churches.

KIT.  A dancing-master; the implements of a burg-lar.

KITE. A letter; fancy stocks.

KITCHEN PHYSIC. Food. "A little kitchen physic will set me up." I have more need of a cook than a doctor.

KITING. Restless; going from place to place.

KITTLE. To tickle; to please.

KITTLER. One who tickles or pleases.

KITTYS. Stock in trade; tools. "The bobbies seized the screwsman's kittys," the officers seized the burglar's tools.

KLEM. To strike. "Klem the bloke," hit the man.

KNAPPED. Arrested.

KNIGHT OF ALSATIA. A person that treats the whole company.

KNIGHT OF THE POST. A fellow that will swear any thing for money.

KNOB. The head.

KNOB-THATCHER. A wig-maker.

KNOCK-ME-DOWN. Very strong liquor.

KNOSE. Tobacco; smoke.

KNOT. A gang of thieves.

KNOWLEDGE-BOX. The head.

KNUCK. A pickpocket.

KONE. Counterfeit money.

KONIACKER. A counterfeiter.

## L

LACE. To beat; to whip.

LACED MUTTON. A common woman.

LACH. Let in. "The cove is bene, shall we lach him?" the man is good, shall we let him in? "If he is not leaky." "I'll answer for him; he is staunch."

LADDER. "He mounted the ladder," he was hung.

LADY. A humpbacked female.

LADY BIRD. A kept mistress.

LAG. A convicted felon.

LAGGED. Convicted; transported.

LAGE.  Water; a basket.

LAGE OF DUDS.  A basket of clothes.

LAID.  Pawned.

LAMB.  To flog.

LAMBASTE.  Flog.  "Lambaste the bloke," flog the fellow.

LAMBO.  To beat with a club.

LAMP.  Eye.  "The cove has a queer lamp," the man has a blind or squinting eye.

LAND-YARD.  The grave-yard.

LAND-BROKER.  An undertaker.  "The cove buys lands for stiff uns," the man purchases land for dead people.

LANTERN-JAWED.  Thin-faced.

LAP.  Drink; butter milk; pick it up; to take; to steal.

LAP UP.  To wipe out; to put out of sight.

LARK.  A boat; a piece of fun; looking for something to steal; on a lark.

LARREY.  Cunning.

LATHY.  Not fat.  "I touched the joskin's skin, but it was as lathy as his jaws were lantern," I stole the countryman's purse, but it was as thin as his face.

LATITAT.  Attorney.

LAVENDER COVE.  A pawnbroker.

LAW.  "Give the cove law," give the fellow a chance to escape.

LAY.  A particular kind of rascality, trade, or profession; on the look out; watching for something to steal.  Sometimes the same as gait.  "What's the cove's lay?"  "Why, you see, he is on the ken's crack"—house-breaking.

LEAF.  Autumn.  "I will be out in the leaf," I will be out in the autumn.

LEAK.  To impart a secret.

LEAKY.  Not trustworthy.

LEAP THE BOOK.  A false marriage.

LEAST.  Keep out of the way; hide; out of sight.

LEATHER. A pocket-book; portmonnaie. "The bloke lost his leather," the man lost his pocket-book.

LEERY. On guard; look out; wide awake.

LEFT-HANDED WIFE. A concubine. It was an ancient custom among the Germans for a man, if he married his concubine, to give her his left hand, instead of the right.

LEG. A gambler.

LEG-BAIL AND LAND-SECURITY. Runaway.

LEGGED. Full-fettered; double-ironed.

LEG IT. Run away; clear out.

LENTEN. Nothing to eat; starving.

LETCH. Unusual fastenings to a door.

LIB. Sleep. "The coves lib together," the fellows sleep together.

LIBBEGE. A bed.

LIBBEN. A private house.

LIBKEN. A lodging-house.

LICK. To coax.

LIFE-PRESERVER. A slung-shot.

LIFT. Help. "Lift the poor cove, he is almost lenten," help the poor fellow, he is almost starved.

LIFTERS. Crutches.

LIG. A bedstead.

LIGHT-HOUSE. A man with a very red nose.

LIGHT MANS. The day.

LIL. A pocket-book.

LILL. A bad bill.

LILLY WHITE. A chimney-sweep; a negro.

LIMB. A lawyer, or lawyer's clerk.

LIMBS. A long-legged fellow.

LIMBO. A prison.

LINGO. Talk; language.

LION. Be saucy; lion the fellow; make a loud noise; substitute noise for good sense; frighten; bluff.

LISTNERS. Ears.

LIVE EELS. Fields. "Bill has gone to live eels, to read and write with Joe." *See Read.*

LOB.  A money-drawer; the till.

LOBLAY.  Robbing money-drawers.

LOBSNEAK.  A fellow that robs money-drawers.

LOCK.  Sometimes a receiver of stolen money; a character. "The cove stood a queer lock," the fellow had a bad character.

LOLL.  The favorite child; the mother's darling.

LOLLOP.  Lazy.

LOLLOP FEVER.  Lazy fever.

LONG.  A large price.

LONG-GONE.  Sentenced for life.

LOO.  For the good of all.

LOOBY.  An ignorant fellow; a fool.

LONG-TAILED-ONES.  Bank bills for large amount.

LOPE.  Run; be off. "The cove loped down the dancers, and got off with the wedge-feeders," the thief leaped down the stairs, and got away with the silver spoons.

LORD LOVEL.  A spade or shovel.

LOUNGE.  The prisoner's box in a criminal court.

LOWING-LAY.  Stealing cattle, oxen, or cows.

LOWRE.  Coin.

LOW TIDE.  Very little money left.

LUGGER.  A sailor.

LUGS.  Ears.

LULLABY KID.  An infant.

LULLIES.  Wet linen.

LULLIE-PRIGGERS.  Thieves who rob clothes-lines.

LUMBS.  Too many; too much.

LUMP.  To beat. "Lump the booby," flog the fool.

LUMP OF LEAD.  A bullet; sometimes the head.

LUMPING THE LIGHTER.  Transported.

LUMBER.  To walk; to walk in a careless, unconcerned manner.

LUMBER.  To receive stolen property from a thief for safe keeping, or disposing of it for his benefit.

LUMBERER.  A pawnbroker.

LUMBERER CRIB.  A pawnbroker's shop.

LUN.  The funny fellow; a clown.

LUNAN.  A girl.

LURCH.  Abandon.  "Lurch the booby, he has leaked his insides out to the coppers," abandon the fool, he has told the officers all he knows.

LURRIES.  Valuables; watches; rings; money.

LUSH.  Drink.

LUSHINGTONS.  Drunken men.

LUSHY.  Drunk.  "The bang-up kiddies had a spree, and got bloody lushy," the dashing boys had a party, and got very drunk.

LUSTRES.  Diamonds.

LYE.  Urine.

# M

MAB.  A harlot.

MACE COVE.  A false pretense man; a swindler; "On the mace," to live by swindling.

MADAME.  A kept mistress.

MADAM RHAN.  A bad woman; a strumpet.

MADE.  Stolen.  "The copper asked me where I made the benjamin.  I told him I didn't make it, but got it on the square," the officer asked me where I stole the coat, and I told him that I did not steal t, but got it honestly.

MAD TOM.  A fellow who feigns to be foolish.

MADGE.  Private places.

MAGG.  A half-cent.

MAGGING.  Getting money by cheating countrymen with balls, patent safes, etc., etc.

MAGSMEN.  Fellows who are too cowardly to steal, but prefer to cheat confiding people by acting upon their cupidity.

MAKE HIM SWIM FOR IT.  Cheat him out of his share.

MANDERER.  A beggar.

MAN-TRAP.  A widow.

MARKING.  Observing; taking notice.

MARRIED.  Two fellows handcuffed together.

5*

MATER. Mother.

MAUDLING. Crying.

MAULD. Very drunk.

MAUNDING. Asking alms; soliciting.

MAWKS. A slattern.

MAWLEY. Hand. "Tip us your mawley," tip us your hand.

MAX. Gin; intoxicating liquor.

MAZZARD. The face.

MEASURE. To examine closely. "The copper snapped and measured me, but could not drop to my chant or mug, and so he turned me up, and I moved my beaters like a bull," the officer examined me, but could not recollect my name or face, and then let me go, and I moved my boots like a locomotive.

MEDLAR. A fellow that smells bad.

MELLOW. Good-natured; a little intoxicated.

MELT. To spend money. "The cove melted a finniff in lush before we parted," the fellow spent five dollars for drink before we parted.

MERKIN. Hair-dye.

MESTING. Dissolving; melting.

MIDDLE-PIECE. The stomach.

MILCH COW. A man that is easily cheated out of his money.

MILKY. White.

MILKY DUDS. White clothes.

MILL. The treadmill; a fight; a chisel.

MILL DOSE. Working in prison.

MILLING COVE. A pugilist. "How the milling cove served out the cull," how the boxer beat the man.

MILL LAY. Breaking into houses; on the crack.

MILLER. A fighter.

MILL THE GLAZE. Break the window. A young thief who had turned State's evidence gave his testimony to the officer as follows: "Jack and Sneaky bustled in front of the jigger. Jack dingged Sneaky's castor into the crib; Sneaky brushed to get it;

Jack pulled the jigger to, and Smasher milled the glaze, touched the swag, and mizzled like a bull, and, ye see, I played shady to pipe the bloke what was done," Jack and Sneaky pretended to scuffle in front of the shop-door. Jack pulled off Sneaky's hat and threw it into the store; Sneaky rushed in to get it; Jack, in the meantime, pulled the door to. Smasher broke the window, stole the jewelry, and was off like a locomotive. I remained near by to watch and see what steps the man would take to recover his property.

MILL TOG. A shirt.

MILKEN. A house-breaker.

MINNIKON. Very small.

MINT. Plenty of money.

MISCHIEF. A man with his wife on his back.

MISS. A mistress.

MISH. A shirt.

MISH-TOPPER. A coat or petticoat.

MIX-METAL. A silver-smith.

MIZZLE. Go; run; be off.

MOABITES. Constables.

MOBILITY. The mob; opposition to nobility.

MOBS. A number of thieves working together.

MOEY. A petition. A convict would say to another: "My pals have got up a bene moey to send to the head bloke, and if it comes off rye buck, I shall soon vamose from the stir; but if it should turn out a shise, then I must do my bit," my partners have got up a good petition to send to the Governor, and if it turns out well, I shall soon leave the prison; but if it should be good for nothing, I must stay my time out.

MOHAIR. An upholsterer.

MOIETY. Fifty.

MOKE. A negro.

MOLL. A woman.

MOLL BUZZER. A thief that devotes himself to picking the pockets of women.

MOLLEY. A miss; a young woman; an effeminate fellow; a sodomite.

MOLL-SACK. Reticule.

MONDONGO. Filthy; full of stench, it stinks beyond the power of endurence.

MONEKER. A name.

MONEY. A private place.

MOON. One month; thirty days' imprisonment. "The poor cove was done for two stretches and six moons," the poor fellow was sentenced for two years and six months.

MOON-EYED HEN. A squinting prostitute.

MORNING DROP. The gallows. "He napped the Governor's stiff, and escaped the morning drop," he received the Governor's pardon, and escaped the gallows.

MORRIS. Move off; dance off.

MORT. A woman.

MOSES. A man that fathers another man's child for a consideration.

MOSH. Dining at an eating-house and leaving without making payment.

MOSS. Money. "A rolling stone gathers no moss."

MOPSEY. A short dowdy woman.

MOPUSSES. Money.

MOOSE-FACE. A rich, ugly-faced man; a poor but handsome young girl who marries an old, wrinkle-faced, ill-looking rich man, is said to have married a moose-face.

MOUNT. To give false testimony.

MOUNTER. Men who give false bail; or who, for a consideration, will swear to any thing required.

MOUNTERS Fellows who hire clothes to wear for a particular occasion; those who wear second-hand clothes.

MOUSE. Be quiet; be still; talk low; whisper; step light; make no noise; softly.

MOUTH. A noisy fellow; a silly fellow.

MOUTH IT. Speak loud.

MOUTHING. Crying. "The mort is mouthing," the girl is crying.

MOVED. Bowed to. "The swell moved to the Moll as they crossed," the gentleman bowed to the girl as they passed each other.

MOW. To kiss. "The bloke was mowing the molly," the man was kissing the girl.

MUCK. Money.

MUCK-WORM. A miser.

MUD. A fool.

MUFFLERS. Boxing-gloves.

MUG. The face; a simple fellow.

MULL. To spend money.

MUM. Say nothing; nothing to say.

MUMMER. The mouth.

MUMPERS. Beggars.

MUND. Mouth.

MUNG. To solicit; to beg.

MUNS. The face. "Tout the mab's muns," look at the woman's face.

MUSH. An umbrella.

MUSHROOM-FAKERS. Umbrella hawkers.

MUSIC. The verdict of a jury when they find "not guilty."

MUSS. A quarrel; a row.

M T. Empty. "The bloke's leather was M T," the man's pocket-book had nothing in it—was empty.

MY UNCLE. A pawnbroker.

# N

NABBED. Arrested.

NABCHEAT. A hat.

NABGIRDER. A bridle.

NABS. Coxcombs.

NACKY. Ingenious.

NAIDER. Nothing; can't have it.

NAILED. Fixed; secured; taken; arrested.

NAMASED.   Ran away ; got out of sight ; ran.

NAP.   To cheat.

NAPPER.   A cheat ; a thief ; the head.

NARP.   A shirt.

NARY.   Not.   "I frisked the joskin's sacks, but nary red was there," I searched the countryman's pockets, but not a cent was there.

NASK.   A prison.

NATTY KIDS.   Young thieves ; smart, well-dressed youngsters.

NATURAL.   Not fastidious ; a liberal, clever fellow. "The bloke is very natural," the fellow is very liberal.

NAZY.   Drunken.

NAZY COVES.   Drunken fellows.

NAZY NOBS.   Drunken coxcombs or fops.

NEB.   The face.

NECKWEED.   Hemp.

NED.   A ten-dollar gold piece.

NEDDY.   A slung-shot.

NEGLIGEE.   A woman with nothing on but her shift.

NEMAN.   Stealing.

NERVE.   Courage ; endurance ; staunch.

NESCIO.   No ; I know not ; can't say.

NETTLED.   Diseased.

NEW LIGHT.   New coin ; new money.

NIB.   The mouth.

NICK.   To cut.   "The knuck nicked the bloke's kicks into the bottom of his poke, and the dummy fell into his mauley," the pickpocket cut through the man's pants into the bottom of his pocket, when the pocket-book dropped into his hand.   This mode of stealing is only practised by the artists of the fraternity.

NICKEY.   The devil ; " Old Nick."

NIDERING.   Bad ; without mitigation of any kind.

NIG.   To clip.

NIL.   Nothing.

NIM.   To steal.

NIMENOG. A very silly fellow.

NIPPERS. An instrument for turning a key on the outside of the door, used by hotel-thieves.

NIPPERED. Turning a key in the inside of a door, from the outside, with a peculiar pair of forceps or nippers. Hotel-thieves use nippers to enter rooms after the inmates have gone to sleep.

NIPPER-KIN. A tumbler; a drinking vessel.

NIQUE. Contempt; don't care.

NISH. Keep quiet; be still.

NIX. Nothing.

NOB. One who stands at the head; a king; a man of rank.

NOBLERS. Confederates of thimble-riggers, who appear to play, to induce the flats to try their luck with the "little joker."

NOCKY BOY. A simpleton.

NOD. Asleep. "Gone to the land of Nod," gone to sleep.

NODDLE. An empty-pated fellow; a fool; the head of an animal.

NONSENSE. Melting butter in a wig.

NOOSED. Married.

NOPE. A blow.

NOSE. A spy; one who informs. "His pal nosed, and the bene cove was pulled for a crack," his partner informed against him, and the good fellow was arrested for burglary.

NOSEMY. Tobacco.

NOTCH. A pocket.

NOTE. A singer.

NOUSE-BOX. The head.

NOZZLE. A chimney.

NUB. The neck.

NUBBING. Hanging.

NUBIBUS. In the clouds. "Blow a nubibus," make a smoke.

NUG. Dear. "My nug," my dear.

NULL. To flog.

NUMS.  Sham; not real.

NYPPER.  A cut-purse, so called by a person named Wotton, who in the year 1585, kept in London an academy for the education and perfection of rogues in the art of abstracting purses and pocket-books. At that period persons wore their purses at their girdles.  Cutting them was a branch of the light-fingered art, which is now out of use, though the name remains.  Instruction in the practice of this art was given as follows: A purse and a pocket were separately suspended, attached to which, both around and above them, were small bells; each contained counters, and he who could withdraw a counter without causing any of the bells to ring, was adjudged to be a " Nypper."  A nypper was a pick-purse; a pick-pocket was called a " Foyster."

## O

OAF.  A silly fellow.

OAFISH.  Simple.

OAK.  Strong; rich; good reputation.

OAK TOWEL.  An oaken cudgel.

OAR.  Meddle with.

OCCUPY.  To wear.  " The cove occupies the oaf's benjamin," the fellow wears the silly man's coat.

OCHIVES.  Bone-handled knives.

OCHRE.  Money.

OFFICE.  Information conveyed by a look, word, or in any way by which the person receiving it is in-telligibly impressed.  " The cove tipped the office, and I was fly to the cop," the fellow gave me the hint, and then I knew it was a policeman.

OFFICING.  Signalizing; a preconcerted signal by a confederate.

OGLES.  The eyes.

OGLE THE COVE.  Look at the fellow.

OIL OF BARLEY.  Strong beer.

O. K.  All right; " Oll kerect."

OLD. Death.

OLD DOSS. The Tombs.

OLD TOAST. A smart old man.

OLD ONE. The Devil.

OLD POGER. The Devil.

OLD SHOE. Good Luck.

OLIVER. The moon.

OLIVER'S SKULL. A chamber-pot.

OLLI COMPOLLI. The chief rogue; a very smart thief.

ON A STRING. To send a person to look for something that you are sure is in some other place, is putting him on a string, or humbugging, fooling him.

ON HIS MUSCLE. "The fellow travels on his muscle," he presumes on his abilities to fight.

ON IT. "On the cross," getting a living by other than honest means.

ON THE MUSCLE. On the fight; a fighter; a pugilist.

ON THE MACE. Ready to cheat; cheating for a living; a professional cheat.

ON THE SHARP. Persons who are well acquainted with the mysteries of gaming, and therefore not easily cheated.

ON THE SHALLOW. Half-naked.

OPTIME. Class. "He's optime No. one as a screws-man," he is a first-class burglar.

ORACLE. To plan a robbery or any kind of deceit.

ORGAN. Pipe. "Will you lush and cock an organ with me, my bene cove?" will you drink and smoke a pipe with me, my good fellow?

OSTLER. House thief.

OTTOMISED. To be dissected. "The bene cove was scragged, ottomised, and put in a glass case for oafs to ogle," the good fellow was hung, dissected, and put in a glass case for fools to gaze at.

OTTOMY. A skeleton.

OUTS. Ex-officers.

6

OUT-AND-OUT. A spree; a frolic.

OUT-AND-OUTER. Distinguished; first-class.

OUTSIDER. Not in the secret; not of our party.

OUTSIDE PAL. The thief that watches outside when his confederates are working within.

OUTSIDE PLANT. A sly place in which the receiver generally keep his goods after purchasing.

OVEN. A large mouth. "The bloke should be a baker—twig his oven," the man should be a baker —look at his big mouth.

OWLS. Women who walk the streets only at night.

OWLERS. Smugglers.

O YES. To cry out. "The O yes of beef was rushing out of his oven like steam from a bull," the cry of stop thief was rushing out of his big mouth like steam from a locomotive.

# P

PACKET. A false report.

PAD. A street; highway, "To go on the pad," to go on the street.

PAD THE HOOF. Walk the street; to be off.

PADDING KEN. A lodging-house.

PAIR OF WINGS. A pair of oars.

PALAVER. Talk; flattery; conference.

PAL. A companion; the partner of a thief.

PALLIARDS. Female mendicants who beg with a number of children, borrowing from others of the same fraternity if they have not enough of their own, giving an opiate to one to make it sleep, pinching and sticking pins into another to make it cry, and making artificial sores on the arms, hands, and face of a third, all to move the hand of the benevolent from their purses to the outstretched hand of the beggar.

PALLING IN. A connection formed by a male and female thief to steal and sleep together.

**PALM.** To fee or bribe.

**PALMER.** A thief that adroitly slips jewelry from the top of a show-case into his pocket.

**PAM.** A knave.

**PANNAM.** Bread.

**PANNY.** A house. " The cove done the panny," the fellow robbed the house; " the cops frisked my panny and nailed my screws," the officers searched my house and seized my picklocks, or false keys.

**PANTER.** The heart. " The lead reached the poor cove's panter, and so there was nothing to be done but to give him a ground sweat," the bullet entered the poor fellow's heart, and all that we had then to do was to put him in the grave.

**PANEL-CRIB.** A place especially and ingeniously fitted up for the robbery of gentlemen who are enticed thereto by women who make it their business to pick up strangers. Panel-cribs are sometimes called badger-cribs, shakedowns, touch-cribs, and are variously fitted for the admission of those who are in the secret, but which defy the scrutiny of the uninitiated. Sometimes the casing of the door is made to swing on well-oiled hinges which are not discoverable in the room, while the door itself appears to be hung in the usual manner, and well secured by bolts and lock. At other times the entrance is effected by means of what appears to be an ordinary wardrobe, the back of which revolves like a turn-style on pivots in the middle above and below. When the victim has undressed himself and got into bed with the woman, the thief enters, and picking the pocket-book out of the pocket, abstracts the money, and supplying its place with a small roll of paper, returns the book to its place. He then withdraws, and coming to the door raps and demands admission, calling the woman by the name of wife. The frightened victim, springing out of bed, dresses himself in a hurry, feels his pocket-book in its proper place, and escapes through an-

other door, congratulating himself on his happy
deliverance. He soon, however, finds out that he
has been victimized, and not unfrequently tells the
story of his loss and shame to the police; while
others, minus their cash, pocket the dear-bought
experience.

PANEL-THIEF.   One who fits up a place for the purpose of robbing men that are brought to the panel-
crib by women who are trained to pick up gentlemen that are on a visit to the city on business or
pleasure.  They endeavor to select those who are
not likely to remain and prosecute the thieves that
have robbed and duped them of their money. ·

PANZY.   A burglar.

PAPER-SKULL.   A thin-skulled fellow.

PAP LAP.   An infant.  "He is but a pap lap," he
is but a baby.

PARCHMENT.   A ticket of leave.  "The cove has
his parchment," the man has his ticket of leave.

PARCHMENT COVES.   Ticket-of-leave men.

PARELL.   To make clear.

PARNEY.   A ring.

PARK RAILING.   The teeth.

PARSON.   A guide-post.

PARTIAL.   Putting one's hand into another man's
pocket; stealing.

PASH.   Price; cost.

PATE.   The head.

PATTER.   To talk.  "How the Moll lushes her jockey
and patters," how the girl drinks her gin and talks.

PATTERED.   Tried in a court of justice.  "The wire
was pattered for drawing a skin from a bloke's poke,
who buffed him home, and of course his godfathers
named him, and the beak slung him for five stretchers and a moon," the pickpocket was tried for stealing a purse from the man's pocket, who caught him
in the act, and of course the jury convicted him,
and the judge sentenced him for five years and a
month.

PATRICO. One who in olden time used to marry persons by placing the man on the right hand side and the woman on the left side of a dead animal. Causing them to join hands, he commanded them to live together till death did them part, and so, shaking hands, the wedding was ended.

PAUM. To conceal in the hand. "To paum pennyweights," to steal rings or any kind of jewelry by working it with the fingers under the palm of the hand, and then up the sleeve or into a pocket. These fellows are called paum-coves.

PAW. The hand or foot. "The fore-paw hand;" "the hind paw foot."

PEACH. To inform; "to turn stag;" to blow the gab; to squeal or squeak.

PEAK. Lace goods.

PEAL. A ball.

PEAR. To draw supplies from both sides; to give the officers information, and then tell the thieves to get out of the way.

PEAR-MAKING. The act of drawing supplies from both sides. *See Pear.*

PECCAVI. I have sinned; I am wrong; a confession of wrong.

PECK. Food.

PECK AND BOOZE. Food and drink.

PECKISH. Hungry.

PECULIAR. A mistress.

PED. A basket.

PEDDLER'S PONY. A walking-stick.

PEEL. Strip; undress.

PEEPER. A spy-glass; an opera-glass; a looking-glass. "Track up the dancers and pike with the peeper," jump up stairs and run off with the looking-glass.

PEEPERS. Eyes.

PEEPING TOM. A curious, prying fellow, who minds other people's business more than his own.

PEEPY. Drowsy.

6*

PEER.   To look cautiously about ; to be circumspect ;
careful.

PEERY.   Suspicious.   "The bloke's peery," the man
suspects something.   "There's a peery, 'tis snitch,"
we are observed, nothing can be done.

PEGTANTRUM.   Dead.

PELT.   A passion ; rage.   "What a pelt the cull is
in," what a passion the fellow is in.

PENNYWEIGHT.   Jewelry ; gold and silver trinkets.

PEPPERY.   Warm ; passionate.

PERSUADERS.   Spurs.   "The kiddy clapped his
persuaders to his prad, but it was no go, the trap
boned him," the highwayman spurred his horse hard,
but the officer seized him.

PETER.   A portmanteau ; a travelling-bag ; a trunk ;
an iron chest ; a cash-box.

PETER-BITER.   A man who steals baggage at hotels,
railroad depots, and from the back of coaches.

PHARO.   Strong malt liquor.

PHARSE.   The eighth part.

PHILISTINES.   Police officers ; officers of justice.

PHIZ.   The face.   "A rum phiz," an odd face.

PHYSOG.   The face.

PICAROON.   A sharper ; a rogue.

PICKLE.   A smart fellow.

PICKLING.   Stealing ; petit larceny.

PICKLING-TUBS.   Shoes and boots.

PICTURE-FRAME.   The gallows.

PIECE.   A prostitute.

PIG.   A police officer.   "Floor the pig and bolt,"
knock down the officer and run away.

PIGEON.   A thief that joins in with other thieves to
commit a crime, and then informs the officer, who he
pigeons for ; and for this service the officer is supposed to be *occasionally* both deaf and blind.

PIG'S EYES.   Small eyes.

PIG'S FOOT.   A jimmy cloven at one end like a pig's
foot.

PIG TOGETHER. Sleep together, two or more in a bed.

PIG WIDGEON. A simple fellow.

PIKE. To run away ; to pike off.

PILCHER. A stealer; generally applied to fellows who steal pocket-handkerchiefs.

PILGARLIC. I ; myself. " There was no one with him but Pilgarlic," he was alone.

PIMP. A boarding-house runner; an attaché of a bawdy-house.

PIMPLE. The head.

PIN. To drink one's allotted share.

PINNED. Arrested.

PINS. Legs.

PIN-BASKET. The youngest child ; the baby.

PINCH. To steal.

PINCHED. Arrested.

PINCHERS. Sometimes called " Exchangers ;" fellows who go into stores or exchange offices with a twenty-dollar gold coin and ask to have it changed for bank bills, and after receiving the bills, suddenly pretend to have changed their minds, and, handing the bills back again, make very profuse apologies for the trouble they have given, etc., etc. The man during the short time that he had the money in his possession, contrived to change bad bills for some of the good ones.

PINK. To stab.

PINKED. Stabbed.

PINKED BETWEEN THE LACINGS. Convicted by reason of perjury. A man encased in steel or iron is only vulnerable at those parts where his corselet is laced ; and hence when an honest man is convicted of a false charge by a treacherous advantage of some weak point, he is said to be " pinked between the lacings."

PIN-MONEY. Money received by a married woman for prostituting her person.

PINNIPE. A crab.

PINNIPED. Sideways; crab-fashion.

PIPER. A short-winded person; a broken-winded horse.

PIPING. Following; trailing; dogging; looking after; watching.

PIT. A pocket.

PLAIUL. Go home.

PLANT. To bury; to conceal. Stolen goods are said to be planted when they are concealed. "Plant your wids and stow them," be careful what you say.

PLANTER. One who hides stolen property.

PLANTING. Hiding; concealing.

PLASTIC. A model artist.

PLATE. Money.

PLATE OF MEAT. A street or highway.

PLAYED OUT. Exhausted; expended.

PLAYTHINGS. Burglar's tools.

PLUCK. To pull.

PLUCK THE RIBBON. Pull the bell.

PLUMB. Honest; upright; good.

PLUMBY. It is all right, or as it should be; we have plenty; they have enough.

PLUMP. Rich; plenty of money. "A plump skin," a full purse.

PLYER. A crutch.

POGY. Drunk.

POINT. To pay.

POKE. A pocket; a purse.

POLISHER. One who is in prison. "The cove polishes the people's iron with his eyebrows," the fellow looks out of the grated windows of his prison.

POLL. The head.

POLL HIM. Get hold of the property, and then refuse to pay for it.

POLT. A blow. "Lend the pam a polt in the muns," give the fool a blow in the face.

POMP. The game. "Save the pomp," save the game.

PONCE. A man who is kept by a woman.

PONCESS. A woman that keeps a man by prostitution.

POND. The ocean.

PONEY. Money. "Post the poney," put down the money.

PONGELO. Drink; liquor.

POP. To pawn; to shoot.

POPS. Pistols. "I popped the bloke," I shot the fellow.

POPSHOP. Pawnbroker's shop.

PORK. To inform the coroner of the whereabouts of a corpse.

PORKER. A saddle. Saddles are mostly made of hog's skins.

PORT ST. MARTIN. A valise; a portmanteau.

POSH. Money; smallest piece of money.

POST. Pay; put up.

POST THE COLE. Pay the money.

POT-HUNTER. A poor person who steals food only to prevent himself from starving.

POULTERER. A fellow who opens letters, abstracts the money and then drops them back into the post-office box. "The kiddy was pulled for the poultry rig," the boy was arrested for opening letters and robbing them.

POUCH. A pocket.

PRAD. A horse.

PRAD-BORROWERS. Horse-thieves.

PRAD-LAY. Stealing horses.

PRANCER. A horse.

PRATE ROAST. A talkative fellow.

PRATER. A hen.

PRATING CHEAT. The tongue.

PRATT. Back parts.

PREMONITORY. The penitentiary.

PRIG. A thief.

PRIGGER-NAPPER.  A police officer.
PRIGGERS.  Thieves in general.
PRIGSTAR.  A rival in a love affair.
PRIM.  A handsome woman.
PRIME TWIG.  First-rate condition.
PROD.  A cart or wagon ; a coach.
PROG.  Food.
PROP.  A breast-pin.
PROPS.  Dice.
PROSPECTING.  Looking for something to steal.
PUFFERS.  Peter Funks.
PULL.  To arrest.  To "pull a purse," is to steal a
purse.
PUNCH.  A blow struck with the fist.  "A punch
in the day-light, the victualling-office, or the halter-
ing place," a blow in the eye, the stomach, or under
the ear.
PUNK.  A bad woman.
PUPPY.  Blind.
PUSH.  A crowd.
PUT.  An ignorant clown.
PUT AWAY.  Locked up ; imprisoned.
PUT A FELLOW UP TO HIS ARMPITS.  Cheated
by his companions of his share of the plunder.
PUT TO BED WITH A SHOVEL.  Buried in the
earth.
PUT UP.  Information given to thieves by persons
in the employ of parties to be robbed, such as servants, clerks, porters, etc., whereby the thief is fa-
cilitated in his operations.
PUT UP JOB.  A job is said to be put up if the
porter of a store should allow a "fitter" to take an
impression of the keys of the door or the safe ; or
when a clerk sent to the bank to make a deposit,
or to draw an amount of money, allows himself to
be thrown down and robbed, in order to have his
pocket picked.
PUZZLE-COVE.  A lawyer.

## Q

QUACKING-CHEAT. A duck.

QUAG. Unsafe; not reliable; not to be trusted.

QUAIL. An old maid.

QUAIL-PIPE. A woman's tongue.

QUAKING-CHEAT. A calf or a sheep.

QUANDARY. What shall I do.

QUARREL-PICKER. A glazier.

QUARROON. A body.

QUARTERED. To receive a part of the profits.

QUASH. To kill; the end of; no more.

QUEAN. A slut; a worthless woman.

QUEEN DICK. Never. "It happened in the reign of Queen Dick," it never occurred; has never been.

QUEEN STREET. "The joskin lives in Queen Street," the fool is governed entirely by his wife.

QUEER. Counterfeit bank bills; base; roguish; worthless.

QUEER. To puzzle. "The cove queered the full bottom," the fellow puzzled the judge. "The bloke queered his ogles among the bruisers," he had his eyes blacked by the pugilists.

QUEER BIRDS. Reformed convicts who return to their old profession.

QUEER BLUFFER. The keeper of a rum-shop that is the resort of the worst kind of rogues, and who assists them in various ways.

QUEER BURY. An empty purse.

QUEER COLE FENCER. A passer of bad money.

QUEER COLE MAKER. One who makes bad money.

QUEER PRANCER. A bad horse.

QUEER ROOSTER. A fellow that lodges among thieves to hear what they have to say, and then imparts his information to officers for a consideration.

QUEMAR. Burn the fellow.

QUES. Points.

QUIDS. Cash; five dollars. "The swell tipped the mace cove fifty quids for the prad," the gentleman gave fifty dollars for the horse.

QUINSEY. Choaked. "Quinsey the bloke while I frisk his sacks," choke the fellow while I pick his pockets.

QUOD. Prison.

QUOTA. Share. "Tip me my quota," give me my share.

## R

RABBIT. A rowdy. "Dead rabbit," a very athletic rowdy fellow.

RABBIT-SUCKERS. Young spendthrifts; fast young men.

RACKLAW. A married woman.

RAG. A dollar. "Not a rag," not a dollar.

RAGGED. Abused; slandered.

RAGS. Paper money. "Poor cove, rags are few with him," poor fellow, money is not plenty with him.

RAG-WATER. Intoxicating liquor of all kinds. If frequently taken to excess, will reduce any person to rags.

RAILS. Curtain lectures.

RAINBOW. A footman; so called from the fact that he wears livery, or garments of different colors.

RAINY DAY. A day of sickness; a day of want; bad times and rainy days.

RAKE. To apportion; share.

RALPH. A fool.

RAMMER. The arm. "The copper seized my rammer, and run me like a prad to the wit," the officer laid hold of my arm, and run me like a horse to prison.

RAMP. To snatch; to tear any thing forcibly from

the person. Pickpockets are said to be ramping a man when a number of them rush on him as if in a great hurry to pass, but manage to run against him, and in the flurry pick his pocket.

RANCAT COVE. A man covered with fur.

RANDY. Unruly; rampant.

RANGLING. Intriguing with a number of women.

RAP. To take a false oath; to curse.

RAPPER. A perjurer.

RASCAGLION. A eunuch.

RAT. A trick; a cheat. "To smell a rat," to suspect.

RATTLE. A hackney coach.

RATTLING COVE. A coachman.

READ AND WRITE. Flight. "He took to *read and write* with Joe in Daisyville.

READER. A pocket-book.

READER MERCHANTS. Pickpockets who operate in and about the banks.

READY. Cash.

RECKON. Cheat.

RECRUITING. Thieves hunting for plunder.

RED. Gold; a cent.

RED SUPER. A gold watch.

RED FUSTIAN. Porter or red wine.

REDGE. Gold.

RED RAG. The tongue. "Shut your potato-trap and give the red rag a holiday," shut your mouth and let your tongue rest.

RED LANE. The throat.

REEFING. Drawing. "Reefing up into work," drawing up the pocket until the purse or portmonnaie is within reach of the fingers.

REGULARS. Share or portion. "The coves cracked the swell's crib, fenced the swag, and then each bloke napped his regulars," the fellows broke open a gentleman's house, sold the goods to a receiver, and each man received his portion.

REP. A man of good reputation.

7

REPS.  A woman of good reputation.

REVERSED.  A man made to stand on his head by rowdies, in order that his money may fall out of his pockets.  It is then picked up as money found.

RIB.  A cross, ill-natured wife.

RIBBON.  Liquor.

RIB-ROAST.  The act of scolding a husband unmercifully by his wife.

RICHARDSNARY.  A dictionary.

RED RIBBON.  Brandy.

RIG.  Joke; fun.

RIGGING.  Clothing.

RIGHT.  All right; just as it was wished to be.

RIGHTS.  "To rights," clear.  "Oh! then, you are *to rights* this time," there is a clear case against you.

RIGHT SORT.  One of your kind; a good fellow.

RHINO.  Money.

RHINO FAT.  Being rich

RING.  To ring in is to join in with another and appear to think as he thinks; to intrude; to force one's self into company where he is not wanted.

RIP.  A poor devil.

RIPPERS.  Spurs.

ROAST.  To arrest.

ROBIN'S MEN.  From Robin Hood.  Expert thieves; grand larceny men; bank robbers, etc.

ROCKED IN A STONE CRADLE.  Born in a prison.

RODGER.  A portmanteau.

ROGUE.  "*Rogue* and pulley," a man and woman going out to rob gentlemen.

ROLL OF SNOW.  A roll of linen.

ROME COVE.  A king; the president.

ROME MORT.  A queen.

ROME VILLE.  New-York.

ROMONERS.  Fortune-tellers.

ROMONEY.  A gipsy.

ROOFER.  A hat.

ROOK. A cheat.

ROOST-LAY. Stealing poultry.

ROPED. Led astray ; taken in and done for.

ROPER-IN. A man who visits hotels and other places for the purpose of ingratiating himself with persons who are supposed to have plenty of cash and little prudence, and inducing them to visit gaming-houses.

ROSE. A secret.

ROTAN. Any wheeled carriage.

ROUGHS. Men that are ready to fight in any way or shape.

ROUGH MUSIC. Noise made by beating old tins.

ROUND. Good.

ROUND ABOUT. An instrument used by burglars to cut a large hole into an iron chest or door.

ROUNDING. Informing; giving information.

ROUND ROBIN. A burglar's instrument.

ROVERS. Thoughts.

RUB. Run. "Don't rub us to wit," don't run us to prison.

RUB US TO WIT. Send us to prison.

RUFFELS. Hand-cuffs.

RUFFIAN. The devil. " May the ruffian nab the cuffin queer, and let the copper twine with his kinchins around his colquarren," may the devil take the justice, and let the policeman be hanged with all his children about his neck. "The ruffian cly you," the devil take you.

RUG. Sleep.

RUGG. It is all right.

RUMBEAK. A magistrate that can be bribed.

RUMBLE THE FLATS. Playing cards.

RUMBOB. A money-drawer.

RUMBING. A full purse.

RUM BITE. A smart cheat; a clean trick.

RUM BLOWEN. A handsome girl.

RUM BLUFFER. A jolly landlord.

RUMBO. A prison.

RUMBOB. A young apprentice

RUMBOSE. Wine or any kind of good drink.

RUMBUGHER. A valuable dog.

RUM CHUB. A fellow.

RUN. Fine; good; valuable.

RUN IN. Arrested.

RUNNING HIM THROUGH. A term used by gamblers when they play with a sucker, and don't give him a chance to win a single bet.

RUSHERS. House-breakers who break into country houses.

RUSTY. Ill-natured. His tongue goes like a door on rusty hinges.

RYBUCK. All right; straight; it will do; I am satisfied.

RYDER. A cloak.

# S

SACHEVEREL. An iron door.

SACK. A pocket.

SAINT GILES BUZZMAN. A handkerchief thief.

SAINT TERRA. A churchyard.

SAM. A stupid fellow.

SANGUINARY. Bloody.

SANS. Without; nothing.

SAWNEY. Bacon; fat pork.

SCAMP-FOOT. A foot-pad.

SCANDAL PROOF. One who has eaten shame and drank after it; or would blush at being ashamed.

SCANDAL SOUP. Tea.

SCARCE. To slip away; to make one's self scarce.

SCAVOIR. Sharp; cunning; knowledge.

SCENT. Bad management. "The cove was nabbed on the scent," the fellow was arrested by reason of his own bad management.

SCHEME. A party of pleasure.

SCHOFEL. Bad money.

SCHOFEL-PITCHERS. Passers of bad money.

SCHOOL. A gang of thieves. "A school of knucks," a gang of pickpockets.

SCHOOL OIL. A whipping.

SCHOOLING. Jostling; pitching.

SCOUT. A watchman.

SCRAGG. The neck.

SCRAGGED. Hanged.

SCRAN. Food.

SCRANNING. Begging.

SCRAPE. Trouble.

SCRAPP. A plan to rob a house or commit any kind of roguery.

SCRAPPER. A pugilist.

SCRATCH. To write; to forge.

SCRATCHER. A forger; a copyist.

SCREAVES. Paper money.

SCREEN. A bank-bill.

SCRUB-BADO. A mean, insignificant puppy; the lowest of the low; *the itch.*

SCREW. A key.

SCREWING. Opening a lock with keys.

SCREWSMAN. A burglar who works with keys, picks, dubs, bettys, etc., etc. ....

SCREWING UP. Choking; garroting. "Screw up the bloke, and that will stop his blasted red rag from chanting beef," choke the man, and that will prevent him from crying "stop thief."

SCRUB. A mean fellow.

SCRIP. Writing-paper. "The bloke freely scratched the scrip, and tipped me forty cases," the man readily signed the paper, and gave me forty dollars.

SCOLD'S CURE. A coffin. "The blowen has napped the scold's cure," the jade is in her coffin.

SCOT. A young bull.

SCOUR. To run away.

SCROBE. A private chastisement.

SCROOF. To live with a friend, and at his expense.

SCROOFING. Living at a friend's expense. Thieves are in the habit of scroofing with an old pal when

7*

they first come out of prison, until they can steal
something for themselves.

SCRATCH. Time agreed upon; to meet at the appointed time; to face another.

SCUTTLE. To cut a pocket.

SEA-CRAB. A sailor.

SEAVEY. Sense; knowledge.

SECRET. Cheated. "The bloke was let into the
secret," the man was cheated.

SEES. The eyes.

SEND. To drive or break. "Take the jimmy and
send it into the jigger," take the crow and force it
into the door.

SERENE. All right. It is all *serene*.

SERVED. Found guilty; convicted.

SERVE HIM OUT. Give him a good thrashing.

SET. Prepared beforehand; "a set thing;" a trap;
a determined thing.

SETTLED. Knocked down; murdered.

SETTLING. Killing. "Settling a bloke," killing a
man.

SETTER. A shadow; an officer in disguise, who
points out the thief for others to arrest.

SHADOW. A first-class police officer; one who
possesses naturally the power of retaining with un-
erring certainty the peculiar features and charac-
teristics of persons, added to the indomitable perse-
verance of the slot-hound to follow his quarry.

SHADY. Quiet; out of sight; not easily found.

SHADY GLIM. A dark lantern.

SHAKE. A prostitute; one who gambles with dice;
to shake; to draw any thing from the pocket. "The
knuck shook the swell of his fogle," the pickpocket
stole the gentleman's handkerchief.

SHAKEDOWN. A panel-thief or badger's crib.

SHAKESTER. A lady.

SHALERS. Girls.

SHALLY. A negative; a person that is never positive.

SHAM LEGGERS. Men who pretend to sell smuggled goods.

SHAP.  A hat.

SHAPES.  Naked.

SHARK.  A custom-house officer.

SHARP.  A man that is well posted; one who "knows a thing or two;" a gambler.

SHARPER.  One who obtains goods or money by any kind of false pretense or representation.

SHARPER'S TOOLS.  A fool and false dice or cards.

SHAVER.  A cheat.

SHEENEY.  A Jew thief.

SHELF.  A pawn-shop.

SHEEN.  Bad money.

SHELION.  A shilling.

SHERIFF'S BALL.  An execution.

SHERO.  The head.

SHERRID.  Run away.

SHICKSTER.  A woman.

SHIFTING.  Cheating or stealing.

SHIGUS.  A judge.

SHILLEY.  No stability.

SHIN-BREAKING.  Borrowing money.

SHINES.  Gold coin.

SHINERAGS.  Nothing.

SHOE-LEATHER.  A phrase to denote some one is approaching.

SHOON.  A fool; a country lout.

SHOOTING - STARS.  Thieves who do not remain long in one place.

SHOP.  A prison.

SHOPPED.  Imprisoned.

SHOVE.  Pass money.  "Shove the blunt," spend the money.  "Shove queer," pass counterfeit money.

SHOVING.  Passing bad money.

SHRED.  A tailor.

SHYCOCK.  A man who is fearful of being arrested; shy of the officers.

SICER.  Sixpence.

SICK.  Imprisoned.

SIDE-POCKET. A drinking-saloon in an out-of-the-way-place; a resort for thieves.

SIFTING. Examining; emptying purses or pocket-books for the purpose of examining their contents, is called sifting.

SILENCE. To kill; to knock down.

SIMKIN. A fool.

SIMON. A simpleton.

SING. To cry aloud. "The cove sings beef," the fellow calls thief.

SING SMALL. Have little to say for yourself.

SINK. To cheat; to hide from a partner.

SINKERS. Thieves who do not divide fair with their companions.

SINKING. Cheating a partner; not dividing fair.

SKEP. A pocket full of money; a place for keeping money; a savings bank.

SKEW. A cup.

SKEWER. A sword or dagger.

SKILLEY. Prison fare.

SKIN. A purse. "The bloke's skin was full of honey," the man's purse was full of money.

SKINK. A waiter.

SKINNERS. Small lawyers who hang about police offices and figuratively skin their clients.

SKIP-KENNEL. A footman.

SKIPPER. A barn.

SKIT. Humbug; a joke.

SKULL. The head of the house; the President of the United States; the Governor; the head man.

SKY-BLUE. Gin.

SKYCER. A mean, sponging fellow.

SLANG or SLAG. A watch-chain. "The knucks twisted the swell's thimble, slang, and onions, and also touched his leather, but it was very lathy. It only raked a case and a half; the thimble was a foist, but the slang and onions were bene. The altemel of the swag raked only fifteen cases," the pickpockets stole a gentleman's watch, chain, and seals, and also his pocket-book; but there was only a dollar and a half a piece for them in it. The watch was a cheat, but the chain and seals were good. The whole plunder divided gave the thieves fifteen dollars each.

SLANGED. Chained by the leg.

SLAP-BANG. An eating-house; a restaurant.

SLAMKIN. A slovenly female.

SLANEY. A theatre.

SLASH. Outside coat pocket.

SLAT. A half-dollar.

SLATE. A sheet.

SLAWEY. A female servant.

SLICK-A-DIE. A pocket-book.

SLIM. Punch.

SLINGTAIL. Poultry.

SLIPPERY. Soap.

SLOP. Tea.

SLOPS. Ready-made clothing.

SLOUGH. To bow the head.

SLUBBER. A heavy, stupid fellow.

SLUBBER DE GULLION. A mean fellow.

SLUICED. To drink. "The bene cove sluiced their gobs with slim till they all snoozed in the strammel like sounders," the good fellow gave them punch till they slept in the straw like hogs.

SLUICE YOUR GOB. Take a good long drink.

SLUM. A package of bank bills; a low drinking-place.

SLUMING. Passing spurious bills.

SLUMMING. Stealing packages of bank-bills.

SLY-BOOTS. A fellow that pretends to be a fool.

SMACK. To share. "Smack the swag," share the spoil.

SMACK. To swear on the Bible. "The queer cuffin bid me smack the calf-skin, but I only bussed my thumb," the justice told me to kiss the book, but I only kissed my thumb.

SMACKING COVE. A coachman.

SMALL SNOW. Children's linen.

SMART. Spruce.

SMASH. To change.

SMASHER. Money-changer.

SMASH-FEEDER. A silver spoon.

SMEAR. A plasterer; a mason.

SMEAR GILT. A bribe.

SMELLER. A nose.

SMELLING CHEAT. A bouquet.

SMELTS. Half-eagles; five dollars.

SMICKET. A woman's shift or skirt.

SMILE. To drink.

SMILER. A bumper.

SMIRK. A superficial fellow.

SMITER. The arm.

SMOKE. Humbug; any thing said to conceal the true sentiment of the talker; to cover the intent.

SMOKE. To observe; to suspect; to understand.

SMOKY. Suspicious; curious; inquisitive.

SMOUCH. To steal.

SMUG. A blacksmith.

SMUSH. To seize suddenly; to snatch.

SMUT. Indecent.

SNABLE. To plunder; sometimes to kill.

SNAFFLERS. Highwaymen.

SNAGS. Large teeth.

SNAGLING. Stealing poultry by putting a worm on a fish-hook, thereby catching the fowl, then twisting their necks and putting them in a bag.

SNAKE. A fellow that glides into a store or warehouse, and conceals himself for the purpose of letting in his companions.

SNAKED. Arrested.

SNAM. To snatch.

SNAPPED. Arrested.

SNAPPER. A gun.

SNAPPERS. Pistols.

SNAPT. Arrested; caught.

SNEAK-THIEF. A fellow who sneaks into areas,

basement-doors or windows, or through front-doors by means of latch-keys, and entering the various apartments, steals any thing he can carry off.

SNEAKING. Conveying away stolen goods.

SNEAKSMAN. *See Sneak-thief.*

SNEEZER. A snuff-box.

SNID. Six.

SNIDE STUFF. Bad money.

SNITCH. An informer; the nose; a spy.

SNITE. Slap; wipe. "Snite his snitch," wipe his nose.

SNIVEL. To cry.

SNOOZING-KEN. A bawdy-house.

SNOT. A gentleman.

SNOUT. A hogshead.

SNOW. Linen.

SNUDGE. A thief who conceals himself under the bed.

SNUFF. Offended. "To take snuff," to be offended.

SNUG. Quiet; all right.

SOAP. Money.

SOD. A worn-out debauchee, whom excess of indulgence has rendered unnatural.

SOFT. Bank bills; paper money.

SOLDIER. A smoked herring.

SOLFA. A clerk.

SOP. A bribe.

SOT-WEED. Tobacco.

SOUNDERS. Hogs.

SPADO. A sword.

SPANISH. Silver coin.

SPARK. A diamond.

SPEAK. To steal; to take away. "Bob spoke with the toney on the chestnut prancer," Bob robbed the fool on the chestnut horse. "To speak with," to steal from.

SPEAKER. Plunderer.

SPEALERS. Gamblers.

SPEILER. A gambler.

SPEILING. Gambling.

SPICE. To steal.

SPICER. A foot-pad.

SPICER HIGH. A highway-robber.

SPIT. A sword or dagger.

SPLIT. Parted ; separated.

SPLIT CAUSE. A lawyer.

SPLIT ON HIM. Informs against; denounces him.

SPLIT OUT. No longer friends ; quarrelled ; dissolved partnership.

SPOONEY. Foolish.

SPORT. A gamester ; a man fond of racing and gaming of all kinds.

SPOT. To make a note of something you wish to remember ; to look at a person with the intention of remembering him ; to point one out to another as a suspected person, or one to be remembered.

SPOUT. A pawnbroker's shop.

SPRAT. Sixpence.

SPREAD. Butter. "The cove pinched a keeler of spread, and was pulled foul. The beaks sent him to the premonitory for three moons," the fellow stole a tub of butter, and was arrested with it in his possession. The judges sent him to the penitentiary for three months.

SPRINGING THE PLANT. To discover the place where stolen property is concealed ; to remove stolen property from its place of concealment. "When I was in the old doss I told my skinner to see Jack and tell him to spring the plant, fence it, and send me my regulars, as I wanted to melt it," when I was in the Tombs I told my lawyer to see Jack, and tell him to remove the plunder from the place in which we hid it, to sell it, and send me my share of the proceeds, as I wanted to spend it.

SPUD. Base coin ; bad money.

SPUNG. A miser.

SPUNK. Matches.

SPUNK-FAKERS. Match-sellers.

SQUARE. Honest; upright; good.

SQUEAK or SQUEAL. To inform. A thief is said to "squeak" or "squeal" when, after his arrest, he gives information against his accomplices, or where stolen property may be found.

SQUEAKER. A child.

SQUAIL. A drink.

SQUEEZE. Silk or satin.

SQUEEZE CLOUT. A silk handkerchief.

SQUELCH. A fall.

STAG. One who has turned State's evidence.

STAG. To see. "*Stag* the cop," see the policeman.

STAGGED. Discovered; informed on.

STAIT. City of New-York.

STAKE. Plunder, large or small in value, as the case may be.

STALL. One whose business it is to conceal as far as possible the manipulation of his confederate who is trying to pick a person's pocket. The stall places himself either in front, back, or sideways, or by any stratagem attracts the attention of the intended victim. Any thing said or done by which the attention is directed from the true state of the case is called a *stall*.

STALLING-KEN. A house for the reception of stolen goods.

STAMFISH. To talk in a way not generally understood.

STANDING. Purchasing stolen property.

STANDING IN. Bidding for; making an offer; taking part with. "The bloke *stands in* with the cross-coves, and naps his regulars," the man takes part with the thieves, and receives his share of the plunder.

STAMP. A particular way of throwing dice out of the box.

STAMPERS. Feet; shoes; sometimes the stairs.

STARCH. Pride.

STARDER. A receiver.

8

STAR-GAZERS.  Prostitutes; street-walkers.

STARK NAKED.  Stripped of every thing; "skinned by a Tombs lawyer."

STAR THE GLAZE.  Break the show-case; break the glass.

START.  The Tombs.  "The cove has gone to the old start," the fellow has gone to the Tombs.

STAUNCH.  Can not be made to tell; reliable; can be trusted with a secret.  "I say, Smasher, won't the cove squeak if he's pinched and promised by the beak to be turned up?"  "No, not for all the blasted beaks this side of Sturbin.  I tell you he is a staunch cove, and there need be no fear," I say, Smasher, won't the fellow betray us if he is arrested and promised by the judge to be set at liberty again?  No, not for all the blasted judges this side of State prison. I tell you he is a reliable fellow, and there is no fear.

STAY-TAPE.  A dry-goods clerk.

STEAMBOAT.  A term used by gamblers.  *See Indians about.*

STEAMER.  A tobacco pipe.

STEEL.  House of Refuge.

STEPPER.  The treadmill.

STEPPING-KEN.  A dance-house.

STICK.  A breastpin.

STICK-FLAMS.  Gloves.

STICKS.  Pistols; household furniture.

STIFF.  A letter; a written or printed paper; a newspaper.

STIFF 'UN.  A corpse.

STIFLE.  Kill.

STIFLE THE SQUEAKER.  Kill the child.

STINK.  To publish an account of a robbery.

STIR.  A crowd; a fire.

STOGGER.  A pickpocket.

STONE PITCHER.  Sing Sing.

STOP.  A detective officer.

STOP LAY.  Two or more well-dressed pickpockets

go into a fashionable quiet street and promenade singly until they select a person that will answer their purpose; one of them stops the person and inquires the direction to a place somewhat distant. On being informed of the route he should take, he pretends not to exactly understand his informant, who, getting a little more interested in his desire to be explicit, draws closer to the inquirer. At about this point, one or both the others walk up and in an instant the amiable individual is minus some part of his movable property. The above practice is what is termed the "stop lay."

**STOW YOUR WID.** Be silent.

**STRAMMEL.** Straw; hay.

**STRANGER.** A guinea.

**STRAW-MAN.** False bail.

**STRETCH.** One year.

**STRETCHERS.** Horse-racers.

**STRIKE.** To get money from candidates before an election, under the pretense of getting votes for them; to borrow without intending to pay back.

**STRING.** To humbug. "String the bloke and pinch his honey," humbug the man and get his money.

**STRUMMER-FEKER.** A hair-dresser.

**STUBBLE.** Stop it.

**STUBBLE YOUR RED RAG.** Hold your tongue.

**STUFF.** Money.

**STUKE.** A handkerchief.

**STURBIN.** State prison.

**STUMPS.** Legs.

**STUNNER.** Extra; superior; very good.

**STUN HIM OUT OF HIS REGULARS.** Cheat him out of his rights; deprive him of his share of the plunder.

**SUBSIDE.** Get out of the way; run away.

**SUCK.** Any kind of liquor.

**SUCKER.** A term applied by gamblers to a person that can be cheated at any game of cards.

**SUCKED.** Cheated.

SUDSDAY.　Washday.

SUET.　Liquor.

SUGAR.　Money.

SUITE.　Watch, seals, etc.

SUPER or SOUPER.　A watch.

SUPOUCH.　A landlady.

SURE THING.　A term used to denote that the person is certain to be a winner.

SUSPERCOL.　To hang.

SWABLER.　A dirty fellow.

SWADDLER.　A fellow who pretends to be anxious for the salvation of every body, and harangues crowds of gaping knaves and fools in the parks, or any other public place.　The pickpockets generally pay him well for his efforts.　Sometimes fellows who pick a quarrel with a man, beat him, and at the same time rob him, are called swaddlers.

SWAG.　Plunder.

SWAG-COVE.　A receiver of stolen goods.

SWAG-RUM.　Full of wealth.

SWEATING.　Reducing the weight of gold coin by putting it in a bag and shaking it violently for some time, and then collecting the dust which is thus worn off.

SWELL.　A gentleman.　"Swell mob," the well-dressed thieves with good address, who appear like honest gentlemen.

SWIG.　Liquor of any kind.

SWIG-COVES.　Fellows who traverse the country under the pretense of begging old clothes.

SWING.　To hang.

SWITCHED.　Married.

SYEBUCK.　Sixpence.

SYNTAX.　A schoolmaster.

# T

TABBY. An old maid; or a talkative old woman.

TACE. A candle; silence; hold your tongue.

TACKLE. A mistress; sometimes clothing.

TAIL-DIVER. A thief who steals pocket-handkerchiefs from coat-tail pockets.

TALE. The number; quantity; share. "Give him tale," give him his share.

TALLEYMEN. Men who loan clothing to prostitutes.

TANGLE-FOOT. Bad liquor.

TANGLE-FOOTED. Drunk.

TANNER. Sixpence. "The kiddy tipped the rattling cove a tanner for lush," the lad gave the coachman sixpence to get a drink.

TAP. To arrest.

TAPE. Liquor.

TAPPERS. Officers.

TARRELS. Skeleton-keys.

TATTLER. A watch or clock. "To flash a tattler," to sport a watch.

TATS. False dice; rags.

TATTY-TOG. A sweat-cloth.

TEASE. A slave; to work.

TEEHOKOIS. Dogs or dog.

TEIZE. To flog. "To nap the teize," to receive a flogging.

TESTON. A coin with a head on it.

THEATRE. Police court.

THIMBLE. A watch.

THORNS. Anxious; fearful.

THRESWINS. Three cents or pence.

THROUGH HIM. Search him.

THROW. To cheat; to rob; to steal.

THROWING OFF. A term used by gamblers when a capper is the partner of a sucker. The capper can lose when he pleases, thereby throwing the sucker off, as it is termed.

8*

THRUMS. Three-cent pieces.

TIBBS. A goose.

TIBBY. A cat.

TICK. Trust.

TICKRUM. A license.

TIED UP GONNOFFING. Stopped stealing; living honestly.

TIFFING. A good natured war of words.

TILE. A hat.

TIMBER. Matches.

TIME ON THAT. Wait awhile, sir; not so fast.

TIP. Information; give; hand to me; lend. "Tip me your daddle, my bene cove," give me your hand, my good fellow.

TIPPET. The halter.

TIT A horse.

TITTER. A sword.

TIZZY. Sixpence.

TOBBY COVES. Fellows that in the night walk the streets near a river. They stun their victim by striking him with a bludgeon; they then rob him and tumble him into the river. If the body is found, it is difficult to say that the man was not accidentally drowned.

TOBED. Struck on the head and made senseless.

TO BLOWER. One who imparts secrets; to inform.

TO BLOW THE GAB. To confess.

TO BREAK A LEG. To seduce a girl.

TOBY. The highway.

TOBY-LAY. Robbing on the highway.

TODGE. To smash. "Todge the bloke and pad," smoke the man and run.

TOGE. A coat.

TOGS Clothes. "The swell is rum-togged," the gentleman is well dressed.

TO HAVE A GAME DEAD. The gambler has a sure thing, and must beat his opponent.

TOLOBON. The tongue.

TOLOBON RIG. Fortune-tellers.

TOMBSTONES.  Teeth.

TOM-CONEY.  A foolish fellow.

TOMMEY.  Bread.

TONEY.  A simpleton.

TOOLS.  Burglars' instruments.

TOOTH-MUSIC.  Chewing food with a good appetite.

TOP.  To cheat; to trick.

TOPPED.  Hanged.  "The cove was topped for settling a bloke," the fellow was hanged for killing a man.

TOP-DIVER.  A roué.

TOPPING-COVE.  The head man of a party; sometimes the hangman.

TOPPER.  A blow on the head.

TOP-ROPES.  Extravagant or riotous living.

TOP-TOG.  An overcoat.

TOTH.  Rum.

TO TURN STAG.  To turn informer.

TO BE PUT IN A HOLE.  To be cheated by a comrade out of a just share of the plunder.

TO BOUNCE.  To brag or hector; to tell improbable stories.

TO BOUNCE HIM.  To get one's property and refuse to pay for it.

TO RIGHTS.  The evidence is conclusive enough to convict.  "Try all they knew, the coppers could not pinch him to rights—he was too fly for them," the officers were not able to find evidence enough against him.  He was too cunning for them.

TOUCH.  To steal.

TOUNGE-PAD.  A scold.

TOUT.  Look; take notice; remember that.

TOUTED.  Followed or pursued.

TOUTING-KEN.  The bar of a drinking-place.

TOWER.  Rage; very angry.

TOWN-TODDLERS.  Silly fellows easily taken in by the sharpers.

TO YARD KICK.  Coat and pants.

TRACK.  To go.

TRADESMEN.  Thieves.
TRANSLATORS.  Second-hand boots or shoes.
TRAP.  Shrewd ; smart.
TRAPES.  Sluttish women.
TRAPS.  Officers.
TRAY.  Three.
TRIB.  A prison.
TRICKS.  Anything stolen from a person at one time by pickpockets.
TRICUM LEGIS.  A quirk or quibble.
TRINING.  Hanging.
TRINKETS.  Bowie-knife and revolver.
TRISTIS.  Not good.  "The fly kinchin is a tristis canis," the smart boy is a sad dog.
TROLL.  To loaf or loiter about.
TROT.  An old woman.
TROTTER-CASES.  Stockings.
TROTTERS.  Feet.
TRUCKS.  Pants.
TRUET.  Stealing money under pretense of changing it.
TRUMP.  A brave fellow.
TRUMPET.  A vain fellow who has a decided partiality for the letter I.
TRUNDLERS.  Peas.
TRUNT.  Nose.
TRUNKER.  The body.
TRY ON.  To endeavor; attempt it.  "Coves who try on," fellows who live by stealing.
TOGEMANDS.  A gown or cloak.
TWITTOCK.  Two.
TUMBLED.  Suspected ; found it out.  "Tumbled on him," came upon him unexpectedly.  "Tumbled to him," suspected him ; thought it was him.
TUMBLER.  A cart; a lock; a sharper.
TUNE.  To beat.  "Tune the toney," beat the fool.
TURF.  Race-course.  "The knucks work the turf for leather and skins," the pickpockets attend the race-courses to steal pocket-books and purses.

TURKEY-MERCHANTS.  Purchasers of stolen silk.
TURNED UP.  Acquitted; discharged.
TURNING OVER.  Examining.
TURTLE-DOVES.  A pair of gloves.
TWIG.  To observe.  "Twig the copper, he is
  peery," observe the officer, he is watching us.
TWISTED.  Convicted, hanged.
TWO TO ONE.  A pawnbroker.
TYBURN BLOSSOM.  A young thief.
TYE.  A neckcloth.
TYKE.  A dog; a clown.


# U

UNCLE.  A pawnbroker.
UNDER-DUBBER.  A turnkey.
UNICORN.  Two men and one woman, or two women
  and one man banded together to steal.
UNTRUSS.  To let down the shutters of a store.
UP HILLS.  False dice.
UPISH.  Testy; quarrelsome.
UPPER-BENJAMIN.  An overcoat.
UPRIGHT MAN.  King of the gipsies; the head of
  a gang of thieves; the chief of banditti.
UPRIGHTS.  Liquor measures.
UP THE SPOUT.  Pawned.
UP TO.  Knowing.
UP TO SLUM.  Humbug; gammon.
UP TO SNUFF.  Cunning; shrewd.
USED UP.  Killed; murdered.
U. S. COVE.  A soldier; a man in the employ of the
  United States.
U. S. PLATE.  Fetters; handcuffs.

# V

VAG. Vagrant. " Done on the vag," committed for vagrancy.

VAMOSE. Run away ; be off quick.

VAMP. To pledge.

VAMPIRE. A man who lives by extorting money from men and women whom they have seen coming out of or going into houses of assignation.

VAMPERS. Stockings.

VARDY. Opinion.

VELVET. The tongue.

VENITE. Come.

VENUS' CURSE. Venereal disease.

VERGE. A gold watch.

VICTUALLING OFFICE. The stomach.

VINCENT'S LAW. The art of cheating at cards.

VINEGAR. A cloak or gown.

VIRTUE ATER. A prostitute.

VIXEN. A she-fox.

VOWEL. Give your note ; I. O. U.

# W

WAITS. Strolling musicians ; organ-players, etc.

WALL-FLOWERS. Second-hand clothing exposed for sale.

WAME   The stomach.

WARE HAWK. Look out; beware.

WARM. Rich ; plenty of money ; dangerous.

WASTE. A tavern.

WATERED. Longed for. "The cove's chops watered for it," the fellow longed for it.

WATTLES. The ears.

WEDGE. Silver-ware.

WEDGE-BOX. A silver snuff-box.

WEEDING. Taking a part and leaving the balance

in such a manner as not to excite suspicion. When a thief abstracts a portion from the plunder without the knowledge of his pals, and then receives an equal proportion of the remainder, it is called "Weeding the swag."

WELCH COMB. The thumb and finger.

WELL. Not to divide fair; to conceal a part.

WESAND. The throat.

WET-SNOW. Wet linen.

WETTING. Drinking.

WHACK. Share of the plunder.

WHEEDLE. To decoy a person by fawning or insinuation.

WHET. To drink.

WHIDS. Words. "Tip me your wattles, my pal, and touch my whids, or I'll make you whindle like a kinchin," give me your ears and take my words, or I'll make you snivel like a child.

WHIDDLE. To tell or discover. "He whiddles," he peaches. "He whiddles the whole scrap," he tells all he knows. "The cull whiddled because they would not tip him his regulars," the fellow informed because they would not share with him. "The joskin whiddles beef, and we must pad the hoof," the countryman cries "thief," and we must be off.

WHIDDLER. An informer; one who tells the secrets of another.

WHIFFLER. A fellow that yelps or cries out with pain.

WHINDLE. A low cry; a painful suppressed cry.

WHIPE. A blow.

WHIPER. A kerchief.

WHIP-JACKS. Men who pretend to be shipwrecked sailors.

WHIPPED. Cheated out of a share, or equal part of the plunder.

WHIPSTER. A sharper; a cunning fellow.

WHISKER. An enormous lie.

WHISKIN.　A drinking-vessel.

WHISTLER.　The throat.

WHIT.　A prison.　"Five gonnoffs were rubbed in the darkmans out of the whit and piked like bulls into grassville," five thieves broke out of prison in the night, and ran like locomotives into the country.

WHITE TAPE.　Gin.

WHITE VELVET.　Gin.

WHITE WOOL.　Silver.

WIBBLE.　Bad drink.

WIFE.　A fetter fixed to one leg.

WIFFLER.　A relaxation.

WILD.　A village.

WILLOW.　Poor.

WIN.　A cent.

WIN.　To steal; to cheat.　"The sneak tracked the dancers and win a twittock of witcher glimsticks," the thief went up-stairs and stole a pair of candlesticks.

WIND.　Money.　"Raise the wind," get money.

WINDER.　To sentence for life.　"The cove has napped a winder for settling a tony," the fellow has been sentenced for life for killing a fool.

WINGS.　Oars.

WINNINGS.　Plunder; money or goods.

WIRE.　A pickpocket; the fellow who picks the pocket.

WIREHOOK.　A pickpocket.

WISH.　Be off; away with you.

WITCHER.　Silver.

WITCHER BUBBER.　A silver bowl.

WOBALL.　A milkman.

WOBBLE.　To boil; to reel; to stagger.

WOOD.　In a quandary.

WOODBIRD.　A sheep.

WOODEN COAT.　A coffin.

WOODEN HABEAS.　A man who dies in prison is said to go out on a wooden habeas; that is, in his coffin.

WORD-PECKER.  A wit; a punster.
WORM.  To obtain knowledge by craft and cunning.


# Y

YACK.  A watch.
YAM.  To eat.
YAVUM.  Bread and milk.
YELLOW.  Jealousy.
YELPER.  A fellow who cries before he is hurt.
YIDISHER.  A Jew.
YOKED.  Married.
YOKLE.  A countryman.


# Z

ZANY.  A jester.
ZNEES.  Ice; snow; frost.
ZOUCHER.  A slovenly fellow.
ZUCKE.  A dilapidated prostitute.

SCENE IN

# A LONDON FLASH-PANNY.

"Ho! there, my rum-bluffer; send me a nipperkin of white velvet."

"Make it two," said a woman, seating herself on a skinner's knee; "and if Jim don't post the cole, I will."

"Why, Bell, is it yourself? Tip us your daddle, my bene mort. May I dance at my death, and grin in a glass-case, if I didn't think you had been put to bed with a shovel—you've been so long away from the cock and hen club."

"No, Jim, I only piked into Deuceaville with a dimber-damber, who couldn't pad the hoof for a single darkman's without his bloss to keep him from getting pogy."

"Oh! I'm fly. You mean Jumping Jack, who was done last week, for heaving a peter from a drag. But you talked of padding the hoof. Why, sure, Jack had a rattler and a prad?"

"Yes, but they were spotted by the harmans, and so we walked Spanish."

"Was he nabbed on the scent?"

"No, his pal grew leaky and cackled."

"Well, Bell, here's the bingo — sluice your gob! But who was the cull that peached?"

"A slubber de gullion named Harry Long, who wanted to pass for an out-and-out cracksman, though he was merely a diver."

"Whew! I know the kiddy like a copper, and

saved him once from lumping the lighter by putting
in buck. Why, he scarcely knows a jimmy from a
round robin, and Jack deserved the tippet for making
a lay with him, as all coves of his kidney blow the
gab. But how did you hare it to Romeville, Bell, for
I suppose the jets cleaned you out?"

" I kidded a swell in a snoozing-ken, and shook him
of his dummy and thimble."

"Ah! Bell! you were always the blowen for a rum
bing."

" It was no great quids, Jim—only six flimseys and
three beans. But I'm flush of the balsam now, for I
dance balum-rancum for the bens."

Bell here produced a rum bing, which at once made
her popular, and the nucleus of a host of admirers;
for, as it respects money, it is with rogues and their
doxeys as with all the rest of the world. Bell truly
justified the adage, that " What's got over the devil's
back, goes under the devil's belly;" for she gave a
general order to the rum-bluffer, to supply all the lush
that was called for by the company, at her expense;
and thereon there was a demand for max, oil of barby,
red tape, blue ruin, white velvet, and so forth, that
kept all the tapsters in the establishment in a state of
restless activity for the next half-hour.

"Bell, you're benish to-night," exclaimed Knapp,
who probably had a design on the purse, which the
course of events somewhat interfered with.

"Stubble your red rag," answered a good-looking
young fellow. "Bell had better flash her dibs than
let you bubble her out of them."

"Why, you joskin," retorted Jim; "if you don't
stow your whids I'll put your bowsprit in parenthesis.
Ogle the cove, Bell—he wants to pass for a snafler in
his belcher tye, though he never bid higher than a
wipe in an upper benjamin."

"I may bid as high as your pintle, and make you
squint like a bag of nails," replied the intruder, "though
you rub us to whit for it."

"Oh! it's all plummy," said Knapp, "so you may cly your daddles. But come, Bell, let us track the dancers and rumble the flats, for I'm tired of pattering flash and lushing jackey."

"Bar that toss, Jim," said Bell, "for you're as fly at the pictures, as the devil at lying, and I would rather be a knight of Alsatia than a plucked pigeon."

This resolution produced a round of applause, which was followed by another round of liquor—promptly paid for by the lady of the rum bing, whose generosity now so far extended itself, that she withdrew from Mr. Knapp's protection, and, even without waiting to be asked, deposited herself in the lap of him of the belcher tye. She had scarcely asserted her title to the premises, before it was disputed by another fair damsel, who emphatically declared, that if the tenant in possession did not immediately leave that, she would astonish her mazzard with the contents of a "nipperkin of thunder and lightning."

"If you do," returned Bell, "I will fix my diggers in your dial-plate, and turn it up with red."

"Mizzle, you punk."

"Well said," Madame Rhan, "but the bishop might as soon call the parson pig-stealer."

"You lie, you bat. I couple with no cove but my own. But say, Harry, will you suffer yourself to be made a two-legged stool of by a flag-about?"

"Oh! button your bone-box, Peg," replied Harry. "Bell's a rum blowen, and you only patter because your ogle's as green as the Emerald Isle."

"It's not half so green as yourself, halter-mad Harry," retorted Peg; "for you know if I wished to nose I could have you twisted—not to mention any thing about the cull that was hushed for his reader."

On a bench, close by the last speaker, was seated Hitch, a police officer, who appeared to be quite at home with the company, and to occasion no alarm or misgivings; but the moment Peg mentioned the circumstance of "the cull that was hushed for his reader," he rose from the table, drew forth a pair of handcuffs, and tapping Knapp's rival on the shoulder, playfully whispered :

"Harry, my lad, the game's up; hold out your wrists for the ruffles."

"There they are, Mr. Hitch, though I suppose you'll be asking me in a week or so to hold out my gorge for a Tyburn tippet."

These proceedings naturally drew a crowd around the parties concerned; but though all sympathized with the prisoner, and the minion of the law was without any assistant, yet there was not the slightest attempt at a rescue, or even the least disposition manifested by the captive of a desire to escape.

"Only nine months on the pad, and to be up for scragging! What a pity !"

"He's too young—he hasn't had his lark half out; and it's like making a man pay a debt he don't owe, to twist him before he has gone the rounds."

"He'll die game for all that ! Poor fellow ! he takes it like a glass of egg-nog."

"Ah ! Mr. Hitch ! isn't it out of order, and he so green ? You ought to give a chap a year to ripen for the hemp."

"Do, Hitch, give him a little longer rope, and take him in his regular turn. You're sure to have him, you know, when his time's up."

"O ! stubble it, George. Hitch can't, or he would; for he never hurries a cove when it's left to himself."

"That's a fact, my kiddies," exclaimed the officer, who seemed pleased at the compliment; "but the commissioner wants Harry, and so, of course, I must pull him."

"I'm satisfied, whatever comes of it," added the prisoner.

Bell whispered in the officer's ear: "Couldn't you let him pike if I come down with a thimble and ten beans ?"

"A watch and ten guineas ?"

" Of course."

" I might if you paid on delivery."

" Ready's the word."

" Warehawk, then, and follow."

Hitch departed with his prisoner, followed by Bell;
but in a few minutes the latter returned and whispered
to Knapp:

" Your client has slipped the darbys, and his name's
Walker. Here's a flimsy, to lay low and bottle your
gab."

The flash-panny was now in the full tide of successful operation—two thirds of its patrons being about
three sheets in the wind, and none of them perfectly
sober. In one corner there was a mill, wherein the
combatants hit the wall more frequently than they hit·
each other. In another, two blowens were clapper-
clawing each other for a bob-cull, who was seconding
both parties, and declaring that the winner should
have him. Here a snafler lay snoring on a bench,
while a buzman, just half a degree less intoxicated,
was endeavoring to pick his pocket. There, three
cracksmen were engaged in a remarkably animated
dispute on the state of the country. Under almost
every table might be seen a son or daughter of Adam,
luxuriating in the realms of Nod. But the bulk of the
company were amusing themselves in a dance; for
one of the fixtures of the establishment was an Irish
piper, who, by the way, was a little fortune to it, for
every one treated Pat.

The dance was yet in its fullest vigor, when Hitch
returned and called Bell to one of the tables.

" Bell, said he, " I have been looking for you more
eagerly than any of your lovers for several months
past—though I found you at length by an accident.
What have you done with the bloke ?"

" Me, Hitch? Why, I have neither seen or heard
of him."

" Come, Bell, it's no use our wasting time in small
talk. You were with him the last night he was heard
of."

"Not I, faith, Hitch. Bring me the book, and I'll swear No to that."

"How then came you by his super?"

"Blast the super! for I fear it has got me into a muss."

"If I take you to Newgate for it, Bell, it will be apt to get you into a halter."

"Well, then it will save me from the Bay fever, or dying in the gutter; for all such as I am must draw one of the three chances."

"Make me your confessor, Bell, without any equivocation or drawback, and I may stand between you and Jack Ketch."

"But what about the stone-jug?"

"That depends upon circumstances. Is the bloke living or dead?"

"Living, for all I know to the contrary."

"You know all about him, Bell."

"If I do, may I cly the jerk at a drag; be trussed in a Kilmainham garter, and fall to the surgeons."

"Well, it may be so," said Hitch, musing; "for if you knew all, half the world would have known it before this time. However, Bell, you can supply a link or two in the chain of evidence, so give me the particulars; and remember, if you tell me a lie I will smell it as it comes out of your mouth."

Just then the guests of the Crooked Billet were interrupted by an uproar in the street.

"Some swells on a lark," exclaimed lawyer Knapp; "dub the jigger and let them in."

And Jim was right; for on the jigger being dubbed, in staggered four bloods, who were sufficiently top-heavy to be ready for any thing. Two of the new-comers, who prided themselves on "knowing the ropes," while their companions were green from the fens. Immediately on their entrance, this hopeful addition to the convivial party already assembled, began to exhibit their "tip-top education" by squaring off for a fight, pattering flash, and ordering in lush. In fact, they out-heroded Herod, for they proved themselves to be yet greater blackguards than the poor rogues whom they were so emulous to imitate. And yet they were "gentlemen," who would have been shocked at the touch of a mechanic, though they gloried in doing things up nutty, like pickpockets and highwaymen. But they were not such knowing kiddies after all, though they considered themselves bang up to the mark; for suddenly one of them cried out that he had lost his purse; and then they all discovered that they had lost every thing they had which was fairly removable. Thereupon there was a devil of a muss, generally, with vociferous calling for the police. The four fellows who had the four worst hats, exchanged them *sans ceremonie* with the strangers, while a couple of fogle-hunters tore off the skirts of their coats to mend their breeches. To finish their spree, by and by in rushed the police, and, on the charge of an elderly, responsible-looking cracksman, hurried the bloods off to the nearest station-house. What rascally things are policemen! Alas! and alack! just about as rascally as all the rest of the world.

## NUMERATION.

| | | | |
|---|---|---|---|
| 1. Eno. | 1. On. |
| 2. Owt. | 2. Duo. |
| 3. Eehrt. | 3. Tray. |
| 4. Ruof. | 4. Quartre. |
| 5. Evif. | 5. Cink or Finniff. |
| 6. Xis. | 6. Double Tray. |
| 7. Neves. | 7. A Round. |
| 8. Thgie. | 8. Double Quarter. |
| 9. Enin. | 9. A Floorer. |
| 10. Net. | 10. Double Finniff. |

# EXAMPLES.

Tim Sullivan buzzed a bloke and a shakester of a reader. His jomer stalled. Johnny Miller, who was to have his regulars, called out, "cop-bung," for as you see a fly-cop was marking. Jack speeled to the crib, when he found Johnny Doyle had been pulling down sawney for grub. He cracked a casa last night, and fenced the swag. He told Jack as how Bill had flimped a yack, and pinched a swell of a spark-fawney, and had sent the yack to church, and got half a century and a finnif for the fawney.

## TRANSLATION.

Tim Sullivan picked the pockets of a gentleman and lady of a pocket-book and purse. Tim's fancy-girl stood near him and screened him from observation. Johnny Miller, who was to have a share of the plunder, called out to him: "Hand over the stolen property—a detective is observing your manœuvres." Sullivan ran immediately to his house, when he found Johnny Doyle had provided something to eat, by stealing some bacon from a store-door. Doyle committed a burglary last night, and disposed of the property plundered. He told Sullivan that Bill had hustled a person, and obtained a watch, and also robbed a well-dressed gentleman of a diamond ring. The watch he sent to have the works taken out and put into another case, or the maker's name erased and another inserted; the ring realized him fifty-five dollars.

## INTERCEPTED LETTER.

RAED MOT: Ecnis uoy evah neeb ot eht tiw, semit
evah neeb llud.  Mij dna em evah enod gnihton fo yna
tnuocca.  Tsal thgin I dezzub a ekolb dna a retsekahs
fo a redaer dna a niks.  Ym remoj dellats.  A evoc-
ssorc, ohw dah sih sraluger, dellac tuo, "poc gnub,"
os sa a gip saw gnikram.  I deleeps ot eht birc, erehw
I dnuof Mij dah neeb gnillup nwod yenwas rof burg.
Eh dekcarc a asac tsal thgin, dna decnef eht gaws.
Eh dlot em sa Llib dah depmilf a kcay, dna dehcnip a
llews of a yenwaf; eh tnes eht kcay ot hcruhc, dna
tog eerht sffinnif dna a retooc rof eht yenwaf
    Ruoy dlo Llom derauqs flesreh rof a elpuoc fo snoom,
retfa uoy tnew ot tiw ; tub uoy ees a detsalb reppoc
deye-yttuc reh, dna derrettap ylneib htiw reh, dna
desimorp reh ytnelp fo eloc fi d'ehs eson rof mih, dna
ni esruoc, Llom ekil, ehs saw demmab yb mih, dna os,
uoy ees, ehs tup pu roop kcalb Llib, dna eh saw deppoc
ot sthgir ; rof nehw yeht deksirf mih, yeht dnuof a tol
fo egdew-sredeef ni eht ekop fo sih skcik.  Eht
hcnuats-nu sevoc, sa uoy swonk, Mot, si reven drakcab
nev yeht dluohs emoc drarof.  Nev I detnahc roop
S'llib senutrofsim lla no me dias sa woh eh sav a eneb
hcnuats evoc sa reve dellap htiw a eneb ekolb dna
t'ndluohs tnav a wef seirutnec ot esaerg htiv.  Yeht
deppit em, rof Llib, evif seirutnec dna a flah.  Won,
uoy ees, taht si tav I sllac nieb a dneirf, deedni, nev
uoy si ni deen.  Nov rehto nosaer yv I t'nsah detfarg
yletal, si taht eht detsalb yeuh evag ym tnahc dna
gum ; dna ni esruoc, uoy swonk I ma oot yreel ot evig
eht spoc eht egatnavdah revo em.  On erom ta tnes-
erp.                                  NHOJ YELLEK.

# APPENDIX.

———•◦•———

## THE GAMBLER'S FLASH.

WORDS FREQUENTLY USED BY GAMBLERS AMONG THEMSELVES, SOMETIMES
IN GENERAL CONVERSATION, AND SOMETIMES WHILE AT PLAY.

---

### A

A' GOSS.   The card that has won three times in one
deal.

ANTI-GOSS.   The card that has lost three times in
one deal.   It is sometimes called a "hotel."   For
instance, a gambler who has been playing, finally
gets "broke;" but the love of play which from habit
has become a second nature in him, causes him to
linger behind to see the luck of others at the table.
Being "dead broke," he borrows from a brother
gambler money enough to pay his hotel or boarding-
house bill.   While looking on at the game an anti-
goss occurs, and thinking that the fourth time is sure
to win, he stakes the money he has borrowed to pay
the hotel, boarding-house, or washerwoman's bill,
whichever it may be, and he loses.   The exclama-
tion among gamblers would then be, "There goe
his hotel."

ARTIST.   One who excels as a gamester.

## B

BANK. Without a party to play against, there can
be no faro-playing. The player must play against
some body, and that some body is a party of one or
more, who hire rooms, and own gambling instruments. The gambling concern is owned by them,
and the servants, from the negro at the door who
answers to the touch of the bell, to the gentlemanly
"picker-up," are in their pay, and act entirely in
accordance with their instructions. The capital
which the owners invest in this gambling co-part-
nership is called the "bank," but the amount varies
greatly. Some banking concerns are not worth over
$100, while others are worth $100,000. It is sometimes easy to break a bank of limited capital, but
to make bankrupt the other is almost an impossibi-
lity. The necessity of a large capital is apparent.
If four or six parties seated at the table should have
$50 each on the table, and four of the six should
win and the other two lose, then the bank in five
minutes would be $1000 the loser. The bank must
be always prepared to lose a thousand or two of an
evening, they knowing well enough that it will all
come back to them before the game closes.

BANKER. The man who puts the money up to be
played for. The owner of the bank.

BETTER. A party who enters a gambling-saloon,
takes his seat at the table, and commences to play,
is a better.

BETTING ON TIME. This frequently occurs when
the character of a party is such that he can be
trusted to pay the money he borrows or the debts
he incurs. If his character is good in this respect,
then he will be permitted to play after he is
"broke," if it occurs that he should be the loser
when he rises from the table. This is betting on
time. The same thing is done in Wall street every

day by speculating brokers. In Wall street gambling there are the "bulls" and the "bears," the object of the one being to raise stock above its actual value and then dispose of it, while the other party depresses it below its value and then purchases it. Nothing of this sort, however, occurs among the professional gamblers, who locate in Broadway and some of the down-town streets running from it.

## C

CALLING THE TURN. When there is one turn, say 4, 6, and 8, and the player calls 4, 8, the caller loses; but if on the other hand it should be the cards he calls, then he wins, and is paid four to one. When a man calls both, he wins and loses on the same turn. In the last turn the player can win three ways. He can copper, call, and play the winning card. He can double the limit of the game, which is the privilege of the player on the last turn.

CAPPER A man who sets at the table and plays, but neither wins nor loses. He is there only for the purpose of swelling the number of players, so that the game won't hurry through too quickly, thus giving the actual player proper time to consider the game and study the moves he should make.

CAPPER. A man in the employ of the bank, who pretends to be playing against it, and winning large amounts. Some gambling-houses in New-York keep two sets of cappers all the time; one set goes on at ten in the morning and retires at six in the evening, when the night-set comes on. Thus the game is continually going on; no matter when a man entered, he finds the game in full blast, and there never is any necessity to start it because of a fresh arrival. Professional gamblers drop to cappers very quickly. Cappers usually want to make too big bets—that is, make too heavy bets. As a general

10

thing they want to bet with the red checks, which represent $5, putting down ten or twenty at a time.

CASHING. This is getting the money from the bank for the checks or chips, if the player has any left on hand when he stops playing.

CAT HOPP. Is when there is one turn left in the box of the same denomination. For instance, two jacks and a five; or three cards in the box, and two of a similar count.

CHANGING IN. Handing in your money for the chips.

CHIPS or CHECKS. The chips or checks are round fancy pieces of ivory of the size of a half dollar, and a trifle thicker. These represent money, and are received from the dealer to play with in exchange for money. They are much easier to handle, and the dealer can see at a glance how much money is bet on a card. The color of the chips indicate the value they represent. There are three colors, namely, white, red and blue. White chips represent twenty-five cents, or one dollar, according to the house. Red chips represent five times the value of the white chips. Blue chips represent $25, $50, and $100. A hundred dollar chip is the highest "fish" ,as the gambler calls it.

CHOPPING. A card which commences to win and lose alternately, is called chopping, and to commence to lose and win alternately, is anti-chopping.

COLD DECK. This is generally done in short cards, or short games. A pack of cards is shuffled, and just as they are about to be dealt out, another pack is substituted. This is sometimes done by faro-players. The dealer having shuffled the cards, or having got another party to do it, drops the cards at his feet, and lifts the packed cards from a handkerchief on his lap. He calls on Sambo, the darkey waiter, to lift a check at his feet, and thus the evidence of his guilt is carried off unobserved. When cleverly done, the trick can not be discovered. One gambler often plays this trick on another, and hence it derives the expressive name of "cold deck."

COPPER. A card can be played to win or lose, at the option of the player. If he wishes to play any particular card to lose, he places a penny on top of the money he stakes. This signifies that he plays it to lose; hence it is called coppering.

CRAPS or PROPS. A game peculiar to Boston. Sometimes it is played with shells, and sometimes with coffee-beans, but more generally the former, as they can be loaded. If four shells are not at hand, four coffee-beans answer the same purpose. It is a substitute for the dice. Thousands of dollars have been lost on this game, but as it has not received the same condemnation from the moral portion of the community that dice has, Bostonians patronize it. There is no other reason why that city alone should patronize it. The game is so childish, that it is ten times more dangerous than any other, and gamblers have no trouble in "roping in" men to play at it, who would faint with horror at the sight of a pack of cards.

CUE. Is a calculation which confirmed gamblers are guided altogether by in playing. They know that after three cards of one denomination have gone out, they can not be split.

CUE-BOX. The cue-box is an exact representation of the lay-out of the cards on the table. The player, by looking at the cue-box, can instantly see what cards have been drawn from the box, thus relieving him of the trouble of keeping the run of the cards in his head. For instance if four jacks had been drawn from the box, and a player should place his money on the jack, they being all drawn, he could not win or lose.

CUE-KEEPER. The man who keeps the cues or marks, so that a player knows by looking at it, which card is in and which is out.

## D

DEALER.   The party who deals out the cards, receiving generally for his services from ten to twenty per cent of the profits of the game from the banker.
DOUBLE CARD.   Two cards of the same denomination.

## E

EVEN.   The player who trys to make up what he has lost.   Having lost $50, he stakes another $50, perhaps his last, for the purpose of getting back what he had lost, to be even with the bank, or get broke in the attempt.

## F

FLAT.   One who has no knowledge, or an imperfect knowledge, of gambling.   No matter how much a man may know of all the sciences in the world, if he is ignorant of gambling, and should enter a gambling-room, the players would smile and say, "There's a flat," a man who did not know any thing.

## G

GAFF.   The gaff is a ring worn on the fore-finger of the dealer.   It has a sharp point on the inner side, and the gambler, when dealing from a two-card box, can deal out the card he chooses; some, however, are smart enough to do this trick without the gaff.   It is now out of date, and the only city in which it is now in use, is Baltimore.   The gaff has been the initiative idea of tricks of this character, and many improvements, of which it is the foundation, have been discovered by sharpers.

# H

HOCK. The last card in the box. Among thieves a man is in hock when he is in prison; but when one gambler is caught by another, smarter than himself, and is beat, then he is in hock. Men are only caught, or put in hock, on the race-tracks, or on the steamboats down South. In a hock-game, if a man hits a card, he is obliged to let his money lie until it either wins or loses. Of course there are nine hundred and ninety-nine chances against the player, and the oldest man living never yet saw him win, and thus he is caught in hock.

# I

ITEMS. Items derives his name from looking at a party's hand, and conveying to the opposition player what it contains by signs. This is Item's occupation. A looking-glass is sometimes used, sometimes signs which mutes would only understand, and sometimes the signs are agreed upon and known only to the parties interested.

# L

LAMAS. High chips or checks representing $25, $50, and $100. There are no $1000 lamas, for the simple reason that with $100 chips any amount of money can be laid on the table.

LAY-OUT. The "lay-out" is composed of all the cards in a suit, commencing at the ace and ending at the king. These cards are posted upon a piece of velvet, which can be spread upon the table whenever the dealer chooses to open the game. When play has commenced, each player places his stake upon any card he may choose, and as the cards are drawn from the box, his bet is determined.

10*

LEAVING OUT. When a dispute arises, a referee of outsiders or lookers-on, is appointed, to whom the difficulty is referred, and whose decision among professional men is decisive.

LITTLE FIGURE. Ace, deuce, and tray.

LOOK-OUT. The look-out is the man who is supposed to keep every thing straight, and see that no mistake is made, and that the dealer does not neglect to lift any money that he has won.

## M

MARKER. Marking is frequently done in playing the game of faro. It is something put down on the card, a pencil, a knife, or any thing, to represent any amount of money the player pleases. He says: I bet $5, $10, $50, or $100, as it suits him and his finances. This saves him from delaying the game by going through his pockets for the exact money he wants. When the deal is out, he settles.

## N

NUDGE. This is not often practised at the game of faro; it is applicable, as its name implies, to cribbage and similar games. The office of a nudger is to touch an associate with his feet. These touchings are signs, which are denominated nudging.

## P

PALMING. Concealing cards in the palm of the hands.

PARLIEU. Is to allow one's money to lie on the table and double. For instance, the player puts $5 on the table, and it wins; instead of lifting it, he lets the original sum lie—that is called a parlieu.

PICKER-UP. We frequently read of country-men being "roped" into gambling-houses, but this occurs from the ignorance of the reporters, who know nothing of the language used by gamblers and sportsmen. Gamblers of the higher grade in New-York, never use the word "roper-in." It is usually confidence-men, ball-players, pocket book droppers, and others attached to that fraternity. The roper-in takes a man over to Brooklyn or New-Jersey, and is an actor in the swindle; the picker-up takes his man to a gambling-saloon, and there leaves him to be enchanted, enchained, and allured by what he sees. Sometimes he only gives the man he has picked up his card, which will admit him to a gaming-house, where he can play a card of another description. The roper-in and the picker-up therefore should not be confounded.

The picker-up is always a gentleman, in manners, taste, dress, and appearance, and sometimes has the superficial knowledge of a scholar. He is thoroughly informed on all the topics of the day. He has seen New-Orleans, knows all about it, and can talk of the gallant defense made there from behind the cotton-bales. He knows all about the evil results arising out of the agitation of the slavery question. He loves Boston and New-England, for it was there he was born and spent his earliest and his happiest days; it was the cradle and the birth-place of liberty, and the world looked with unreserved delight upon the efforts which the men of the East put forth in the cause of freedom; he has spent many happy years in the far West, its vast prairies, its wide-spread, majestic forests, and mighty rivers, and he can not help warming up when he reverts to these themes, which moved the hearts of philosophers, poets, and statesmen.

This is the picker-up. He first sees the man's name on the hotel-register, and where he is from.

He then sees him out, studies his character, and ascertains his means and the object of his visit to the city; and the picker-up, if smart, reads his victim phrenologically without touching his head. Every man has some weak point which can be played upon, and the duty of the picker-up is to discover it. It does not take him long generally to get a stranger to visit a gambling-hell. Very many of the servants of hotels are in the pay of pickers-up—the duty of the servant being to get information concerning guests, which his employer can use.

PIKER. Is a man who plays very small amounts. Plays a quarter, wins, pockets the winnings, and keeps at quarters; and never, if he can help it, bets on his winnings.

PLAYING ON VELVET. Playing on the money that has been won from the bank.

PRESS. When a man wins a bet, and instead of lifting and pocketing the winnings, he adds to the original stake and winnings, it becomes a press.

PRIVATE GAME. So called because the flat is led to suppose that no professional gamblers are admitted, and thus he is the more easily duped.

PUBLIC GAME. A game where any body can be admitted.

## R

REPEATER. For instance, when a card wins or loses at one deal, and the same thing occurs the next deal, it is a repeater.

ROUNDER. One who hangs around faro-banks, but does not play. In other words, a loafer, a man who travels on his shape, and is supported by a woman, but does not receive enough money to enable him to play faro. Gamblers call such men rounders, outsiders, loafers.

RUSSER. A big player.

## S

SHOE-STRING. When a man bets a small amount and runs it up to a large amount, it is called a shoe-string.

SHORT CARDS. By some called short game. A game of seven-up or cribbage. For instance, "Have you been playing faro to-night?" "No." "What then?" "I have been playing short cards."

SLEEPER. A bet won by the bank or a better, which has been overlooked and lies on the table without a claimant.

SKINNING. A sure game, where all who play are sure to lose, except the gamesters.

SPLIT. When two cards come alike. For instance, if two jacks should come out, the banker takes one half of the money.

SQUARE GAME. When cards are dealt fairly, and there is no cheating.

SUMMER GAME. Playing merely for amusement.

SUMMER GAME. Playing a game for the benefit of another person with his money.

STRIPPERS. Cards cut at the sides for the purpose of carrying on a skinning game.

STUCK. When a man has lost all his money, and is trying on the last throw to retrieve his loss and he is beat, then he is stuck.

SUCKER. A flat; one who can play cards, but does not know all the tricks and traps in gambling.

SUPPER CUSTOMERS. Some of the fashionable gambling-houses have free suppers for their customers; this is done to induce the better class of gambling merchants to patronize the house. But there are some men who frequent these houses and take supper, but never play. When such a one is asked if he is going to take a hand in, his usual answer is, "Thank you, sir, I'm a supper customer to night."

## T

TELL-BOX. The tell-box is an improvement on the

10

gaff, and has a fine spring attached to it.    The object is to cheat the dealer.    The dealer plays with a pack of cards which the player has had a chance to handle, and he rubs the backs of certain of them with sand-paper.    The rough card adheres to the smooth one, and the fact that it does not move a hair's breadth in the box enables him to know the card that is covered, and he plays accordingly.    He can also play in the same manner with a new pack of cards without sanding them, as certain cards re- quire a greater amount of ink than others.

THE POT.    The six, seven, and eight.

TRICKS.    When a player takes the cards from his opponent that counts.    If the queen is put down and king follows, which is higher, then the queen is taken.    That is a trick.

TRICK GAMES.    Such games as whist, where tricks count.

## Z

ZODIAC.    This word has degenerated into Soda.    It means the top card in the box.

## TECHNICAL WORDS AND PHRASES,

# BILLIARD-PLAYERS.

————•————

ATTITUDE.   The position in which the player stands while at the billiard-table, when about to strike the ball.   The acquisition of a good attitude is a matter of first importance to the new beginner.   It is almost impossible to lay down fixed rules in this particular, as the peculiarities of height and figure would render the rules that would be excellent in one case, totally inapplicable in the other.   Perfect ease is the grand *desideratum ;* and this is to be acquired by practice, and a close observation of the best players.

BANK.   When the player makes his own ball hit any of the cushions before striking the object-ball.

BILLIARD-SHARP.   A class of character not tolerated in respectable saloons.   As a general thing, the billiard-sharp is a retired marker, who fancies it is no longer respectable to work for an honest living, but that he is smart enough, and has learned tricks enough at his former business, to enable him to win as much money as he wants from the less experienced amateurs of the game, who figure in his vocabulary as "the flats."   He generally frequents those establishments where one or two billiard-tables are made the stall behind which some dishonest occupation is carried on ; and here he is at home, and in his glory.   He makes himself particularly friendly with any one who will ask him to "take a drink," and in his assumed duties he fills the offices of lounger, runner, talker, player, sponge, shoulder-hitter, and referee.

He is also a runner, and sort of travelling blower to second-rate manufacturers of billiard-tables. These men supply him with clothes, to enable him to mingle in respectable society, and allow him an enormous per centage for every billiard-table sold to a stranger through his agency. In addition to this, it is his business to pull down the reputation of such manufacturers as despise and scorn the means by which he earns his dishonest livelihood. As soon as he has made "a hit" in one saloon, he is off to another, and in this way goes the rounds of the city until all the places which harbor him, are, in his own phrase, "played out."

Such a man is to be avoided as one of the worst species of sharpers. He has a thousand pretenses under which to borrow money, and will act as if quite offended if refused. The stranger should avoid all such men, and especially any one with whom he is not well acquainted, who should ask him to play for any given sum, "just to give an interest to the game."

BOWERY SHOT. When the balls played with and at, are jarred together—a pushing shot.

BREAK. The position the balls are left in after the shot.

BURST. A term chiefly used at pin-pool, when a player has exceeded the number which is placed as the common limit to the game, and must, therefore, either retire from the game, or take a privilege of another life.

CAROM. (French, *Carombolage.*) To hit more than one of the balls on the table with your own. In England this word has been corrupted to "cannon."

COUNT. Is the reckoning of the game. Making a count, is to make a stroke which will add some figures to the player's reckoning.

DISCOUNT. When one player is so much the superior of another, that he allows all the counts made by his opponent to be deducted from his own reckoning, he is said to " discount" his adversary's gains. In "double" and "treble discounts," twice and thrice the amount of his opponent's gains are deducted from the player's score. In no other game but billiards are such immense odds possible. A man of close observation, temperate habits, steady nerves, and large experience, may give almost any odds to an inferior player, and still have a fair chance of success.

DOUBLET or CROSS. When the ball to be pocketed is first made to rebound from the opposite cushion.

FOLLOW. When a player's ball rolls on after another ball which it has impelled forward.

FORCE. When the player's ball retrogrades after coming in contact with another.

FOUL STROKE or SHOT. Any stroke made in violation of the known rules of the game.

FULL BALL, QUARTER BALL, HALF BALL, FINE or CUT BALL, OWN or CUE BALL, and OBJECT BALL. The "object ball" is the ball aimed at; the " own or cue ball" is the ball directed toward the "object ball;" the other terms relate to the position in which the object ball is struck.

GERMANTOWNER. *See Bowery Shot.*

HAZARD. To drive any of the balls into any of the pockets.

HAZARD, DOUBLE. When two balls are pocketed with the same stroke.

HAZARD, LOSING. When the player's ball is pocketed by his own act.

HAZARD, WINNING. When the player pockets either of the red balls, or his adversary's ball.

HAZARD, TAKING A. A term used to express that a player is so confident of making a certain hazard, that he will undertake to do it, under penalty of losing, in case he does not succeed, as many lives as

11

he would have gained if successful. The phrase is most frequently employed in two-ball pool.

HUG. When any of the balls run close alongside of a particular cushion, they are said to hug it.

JAW. When a ball is prevented from dropping into a pocket by the cushions, which extend like jaws on either side.

JUMP. When the player forces his ball by a downward stroke to leap up from the table.

KILLED or DEAD BALL. When a ball in pool has lost its lives, and its chances are not renewed by privileges, it is said to be killed.

KISS. When the ball played with strikes another ball more than once, they are said to kiss; or when two balls, not played with, come in contact.

LONE GAME. A game in which one of the parties is an experienced player, and the other a novice— the former having the game in his own hands.

MISS. To fail striking any of the balls upon the table.

MISS-CUE. When the cue, from any cause, slips off the ball without accomplishing the intended stroke.

PLAYING FOR SAFETY. When the player foregoes a possible advantage, in order to leave the balls in such a position that his opponent can make nothing out of them.

PLAYING SPOT-BALL. When the player is not limited to the number of times he may pocket the red ball from the spot.

PRIVILEGE. When a player loses the lives, or chances, which were given to his ball on its entry into the game, and desires to purchase another chance from the other players, he asks a " privilege."

SCRATCH. When a player wins a stroke or count by accident, without deserving it, he is said to have made a scratch.

STRINGING FOR THE LEAD. A preliminary arrangement, by which it is determined who shall have the choice of lead and balls.

TIMBER LICK. *See Bowery Shot.*

# BBOKERS'

## TECHNICALITIES IN BRIEF.

A BULL is one who buys stocks on speculation, thinking they will rise, so that he can sell at a profit.

A BEAR is one who sells stocks on speculation, thinking they will fall, so that he can buy in for less money to fill his contracts.

A CORNER is when the bears can not buy or borrow
the stock to deliver in fulfillment of their contracts.

A DEPOSIT is earnest-money, lodged in the hands
of a third party, as a guaranty; "5 up," "10 up,"
etc , is the language expressive of a deposit.

OVERLOADED is when the bulls can not pay for the
stocks they have purchased.

SHORT is when a person or party sells stocks when
they have none, and expect to buy or borrow them
in time to deliver.

LONG is when a person or party has a plentiful supply of stocks.

A FLYER is to buy some stock with a view to selling
it in a few days, and either make or lose, as luck
will have it.

A WASH is a pretended sale, by special agreement
between the seller and buyer, for the purpose of getting a quotation reported.

## A HUNDRED STRETCHES HENCE

Oh ! where will be the culls of the bing
   A hundred stretches hence ?
The bene morts, who sweetly sing,
   A hundred stretches hence ?
The autum-cacklers, autum-coves,
The jolly blade who wildly roves ;
And where the buffer, bruiser, blowen,
And all the cops and beaks so knowin',
   A hundred stretches hence ?


And where the swag, so bleakly pinched,
   A hundred stretches hence ?
The thimbles, slang, and danglers filched,
   A hundred stretches hence ?
The chips, the fawneys, chatty-feeders,
The bugs, the boungs, and well-filled readers;
And where the fence and snoozing-ken,
With all the prigs and lushing men,
   A hundred stretches hence ?


Played out their lay, it will be said
   A hundred stretches hence ,
With shovels they were put to bed
   A hundred stretches since !
Some rubbed to whit had napped a winder,
And some were scragged and took a blinder,
Planted the swag, and lost to sight,
We'll bid them, one and all, good night,
   A hundred stretches hence.

## TECHNICAL WORDS AND PHRASES

# IN GENERAL USE BY PUGILISTS.

ABROAD. Confused; staggered.

A GENERAL. Possessed of superior science.

BACK-HANDED BLOW. Striking with the back of the clenched fist.

BARNEY. A fight that is sold.

BEAK. The nose.

BEAM-ENDS. Thrown or knocked into a sitting position.

BOKO. The nose.

BOTTOM. Power of endurance.

BOUNCED. Frightened with stories of another's prowess.

BREAD-BASKET. The stomach.

BUFFER. A pugilist.

CHANCERY. When one boxer gets the head of his opponent under his left arm, and holding him by the left wrist, strikes him in the face with his right hand, severely punishing him.

CLARET. Blood.

CHOPPER. A blow given from above.

COLORS. The respective handkerchiefs that each fights under.

COMMISSARY. The person who fixes the ropes and stakes.

CONK. The nose.

CORINTHIAN CANVAS. A term applied to the *propria personæ* of an English nobleman who is an amateur of pugilism.

COUNTER-HITTING.  When both parties in a fight strike each other at the same time.

CROSS-BUTTOCK.   To get an adversary on the hip, and then throw him.

CUT OF TIME.  Defeated; could not come up to the call.

DADDLES.   The hands.

DOING WORK.   Training.

DOUBLER.   A blow which causes the person struck to bend forward.

DUKES.   The hands.

DUTCH COURAGE.   Cowardice; one who drinks liquor to stimulate his courage.

ENOUGH.   When one of the boxers wishes to discontinue the fight he exclaims, "Enough."

FACER.   A severe blow struck directly in the face.

FEINTING.   Making pretense of delivering a blow.

FIBBING.   Short, quick blows when the parties are close to each other.

FIDDLER.   A pugilist that depends more upon his activity than upon his bottom.

FINICKING FOP.   A dandy or empty swell who makes much ado about pugilism, because he thinks it knowing and stylish.

FINE FETTLE.   In good condition; healthy.

FLABBY.   The flesh in a soft condition.

FLOORER.   A knock-down blow.

FORKS.   The hands.

FOSSED.   Thrown.

FOUL.   An unwarrantable interference on the part of a second to frustrate an opponent's designs.

FOUL BLOW.   A blow given contrary to the accepted rules of the ring; below the belt.

GAME.   Courageous, unflinching.

GAVE IN.   Yielded.

GLUTTONY.   Punishing a man severely, without special regard to the science of pugilism.   One who can endure a great amount of punishment, is called a *glutton*.

GOB.   The mouth.
GOOD-WOOLED.   A man of unflinching courage.
GOT HOME   A telling blow.
GROGGY.   Not able to stand erect from punishment received.
GRUEL.   Punishment.
GULLET.   The throat.
HIGH-COLORING.   Drawing blood freely.
IN DIFFICULTIES.   Nearly defeated.
IN MOURNING.   The eyes blackened and closed up.
IN TROUBLE.   Almost beaten.
IVORIES.   Teeth.
JOLLYING.   Low expressions used by one combatant to the other during the fight, for the purpose of irritating him and diverting his attention.
KNOWLEDGE-BOX.   The head.
LAMPS.   The eyes.
LEARY.   Active ; smart.
LEVELLER.   When one of the contestants is brought completely to the ground.
LISTENERS.   The ears.
MARK.   The pit of the stomach.
MAZZARD.   The mouth.
MENTOR.   A second in the ring.
MILLED.   *See Punished.*
MILLING COVES.   Persons who regularly frequent milling-pannies, for the purpose of exhibiting their skill in boxing.
MILLING-PANNIES.   Places of resort for pugilists in which sparring exhibitions are given.
MITTENS.   Boxing-gloves.
MITTEN-MILL.   A glove fight.
MUSH.   The mouth.
NUT.   The head.
NUT-CRACKER.   A severe blow on the head.
OGLES.   The eyes.
PINS.   The legs.
PLUCK.   Spirit ; boldness ; courage.
POTATO-TRAP.   The mouth.

PUFFED.  Swollen.

PUNISHED.  Severely bruised or cut in the fight.

RALLY.  When the fighters close up and strike promiscuously.

RANTER.  One who makes greater pretension of skill in boxing than he exhibits when engaged in a set-to.

RIB-BENDER.  A forcible hit in the ribs.

RUBY.  Blood.

SHAKE-UP.  A pugilistic encounter.

SHIFT.  When a boxer purposely falls to save himself from a knock-down blow, he is said to make a *shift*.

SLOGGER.  A pugilist.

SMELLER.  The nose.

SPARRING GILLS.  *See Milling Coves.*

STAMINA.  Ability to punish and endure punishment.

TAKE THE SHINE OUT.  To lower the man's self-esteem.

THE CROOK.  Entwining the legs for a fall.

THE SCRATCH.  A line drawn in the middle of the ring.

THREW DOWN THE GLOVE.  Gave a challenge.

TIME.  The breathing-space which, by the accepted rules of the ring, is confined to a given period. "Coming to time," is coming promptly to the line at the expiration of the time agreed upon.

TOLD OUT.  Beaten ; defeated.

UPPER CUT.  A terrific blow struck upwards.

UPPER CUSTOMER.  A term applied to patrons of the ring amongst the upper classes who are not themselves pugilists.

UPPER STORY.  The head.

WHITE FEATHER.  Cowardice.

WIND UP.  The finishing round.